The Descent of Darwin

The Descent of Darwin

A Handbook of
Doubts about Darwinism

———————— ❋ ————————

Brian Leith

COLLINS
St. James's Place, London

William Collins Sons & Co Ltd
London · Glasgow · Sydney · Auckland
Toronto · Johannesburg

First published 1982
© Brian Leith 1982
ISBN 0 00 219548 8

Typeset by
PR Printing

Designed and Produced by
Radavian Press, Reading

Contents

Preface

If I have simplified or polarized the various debates in present-day Darwinian theory it has been in order to clarify the issues for the non-biologist; I trust that this has misrepresented neither the critics, nor the defenders, of the 'faith'.

I thank Professor Sam Berry, Dr Laurence Cook, Robert MacDonald and Laura Zunz for helpful criticism of the script, and Stephanie Burton, and Libby and Kate Tiffin for their work preparing the book.

Introduction

---- ❋ ----

No scientific theory arouses so much interest among the non-scientists as Darwinism. This is hardly surprising; Charles Darwin's simple proposal—that life has evolved through time by means of natural selection—is bound to influence a great deal of our day-to-day life. Darwin's theory purports to explain a staggeringly large part of the world about us: from the delicate balance of a tropical rain forest, to medical questions about the origins of disease, to the motivation behind the intricate behaviour patterns of man. Darwinism is not only an ambitious theory of organic nature—it is virtually a philosophy of life in itself. What is more, the philosophy implied by Darwinism, that life may have no 'purpose' in the traditional religious sense, and that life is ultimately a random process, is certain to provoke attention or even hostility among the non-biologists.

In this way Darwinism is unique among scientific theories. Because it attempts to explain not only events in the outside world but also *man's* origins and his place in those events, Darwinism straddles the gap between philosophy and science, between faith and reason, in a way no other scientific theory does. If we were to discover tomorrow that Copernicus was wrong, that the sun actually does go round the earth rather than the reverse, what would happen? Obviously the physicists and astronomers would have headaches trying to reconcile the discovery with their other observations, but would it change your life or mine? Would we think of ourselves, or the purpose in our lives, in a different way? Probably not.

Not so with Darwinism. If we were suddenly to discover

that life had not evolved after all, or that it had evolved in a fundamentally non-Darwinian way, the effect on our lives would be tangible. Not only would the biologists have to rethink their observations of nature, but theologians, philosophers and probably even politicians would be forced to look afresh at man's place in nature. In the one hundred and twenty years or so since the publication of *The Origin of Species* Darwinian principles have seeped into every corner of our 'world-view'. Why does a baby cry? To ensure its survival. Are all men born equal? No, some are fitter and more competitive than others. Why is there such a thing as altruism? So that the altruist may ultimately be the benefactor. Like it or not, many of the central issues of Darwinism are also the central issues of our culture and politics: over-population, the struggle for existence, the sensible use of resources, and so on. A theory about man's origins is bound to entail more than straightforward science.

It is therefore of immediate concern to both biologist and layman that Darwinism is under attack. The theory of life that undermined nineteenth-century religion has virtually become a religion itself and in its turn is being threatened by fresh ideas. The attacks are certainly not limited to those of the creationists and religious fundamentalists who deny Darwinism for political and moral reasons. The main thrust of the criticism comes from within science itself. The doubts about Darwinism represent a potential revolt from within rather than a seige from without.

What is even more surprising is that these doubts are arising simultaneously from several independent branches of science. With a growth in the appreciation of the philosophy of science—largely due to the influence of the philosopher Karl Popper—has come a doubt about whether Darwinism is, strictly speaking, scientific. Is the theory actually testable—as good theories must be? Is the idea of natural selection based on a tautology, a simple restatement of some initial assumptions? From within biology the doubts have come from scientists in half a dozen separate fields. Many palaeontologists are unconvinced by the supposed gradualness of Darwinian evolution; they feel that the evidence points to abrupt change—or else to no change at all. Some geneticists question Darwin's explanation for the 'origin of species', feeling that natural selection may have virtually nothing to do with the events that lead to the appearance of new species. Among other scientists, for example among immunologists, embryologists and taxonomists, the same feeling seems to be growing: there is a lot more to evolution than Charles Darwin envisaged, and even the modern synthesis of evolutionary ideas—called neo-Darwinism (see Chapter 1)—seems inadequate in many respects.

In some ways the attacks are nothing new; several of the debates now surfacing can be traced to Darwin himself, and even before. What is new is the climate that the debates are creating. Since the days of Darwin and his 'bulldog', T.H. Huxley, and especially since the confident synthesis that created neo-Darwinism in the 1940s, any attack on evolutionary theory has been treated rather like flat-earthism: evidence of mental aberration due to religious mania or political fanaticism. Such attacks were simply not taken seriously. This is no longer true. In the past ten years has emerged a new breed of biologists who are considered scientifically respectable, but who have their doubts about Darwinism.

This book is about these new biologists and the reasons why they doubt Darwin. Why are they questioning the orthodoxy *now?* Are the simultaneous attacks merely a coincidence, or is there some common link? Can the theory which has provided the foundation, and focus, for all biological investigation over the past century weather the storm? Or are we on the threshold of a new theory of evolution?

Chapter 1

What is neo-Darwinism?

———————————— ❀ ————————————

Contrary to popular opinion, scientific theories are not rigid doctrines dogmatically laying down the facts of nature (even though they are frequently adopted by scientists with an almost religious fervour). Good scientific theories, like good scientists, are flexible. They are constantly being updated to accommodate the most recent findings. Although Darwinian ideas may be on the threshold of a dramatic reappraisal, this is not a sudden revolution; Darwinism has been developing as a theory ever since the 1850s, and has already changed markedly from Darwin's original hypothesis.

When Darwin wrote *The Origin of Species* the processes underlying heredity—a concept so vital to evolution—were largely a mystery. While it was commonly understood that offspring resembled parent, there was no underlying concept of inheritance to explain why this should be or why some features—such as eye colour in man—are 'all-or-nothing' in heredity, while others—such as height—are blended and variable. Clearly there was an embarrassing gap in Darwin's theory while there was no convincing explanation of inheritance. It was not until the discovery of the work of the Austrian monk Gregor Mendel in 1900 that the basic rules of heredity were assimilated into biology and Darwinism reappraised to see whether the theory was compatible with the newly found Mendelian laws. Similarly in the early 1950s, with the dramatic advances in molecular chemistry which led Watson and Crick to map the atomic structure of DNA and to 'crack' the genetic code, a reanalysis of Darwinian theory became necessary. In both cases the existing theory was able to absorb the discoveries of genetics without difficulty; in this way the theory of evolution has itself evolved and diversified as an explanation of nature. In some respects Darwin is now known to have been quite wrong—his own theory of heredity was naïve and mistaken—but the central core of his theory remains the foundation of modern evolutionary theory, or neo-Darwinism.

Neo-Darwinism, then, is really just Darwinism that has incorporated the scientific advances of the past century, in particular an appreciation of heredity and DNA. Until the early part of this century Darwinism was considered by most biologists as 'another theory' which had its strengths and weaknesses. Although Darwin had established the idea of *evolution* beyond reasonable doubt, his theory of natural selection as an explanation for evolution was on shaky ground until heredity was fully understood. Once the synthesis had been achieved, evolution by natural selection became the single unifying principle of all biology—and has remained so ever since.

So what is the neo-Darwinian theory of evolution? In order to grasp the significance of the recent attacks and doubts, it is important to set the stage, to outline this great unifying principle called neo-Darwinism which has dominated all biology for more than a generation.

The core of Darwinism and neo-Darwinism is natural selection, or the 'survival of the fittest', the idea that species can originate through the differential survival of creatures in a struggle for existence. Natural selection is seen as the inevitable outcome of three basic facts of life: over-population, variation, and heredity.

First, over-population: plants and animals tend to produce more offspring than can survive. A pair of mice, for example, can produce a litter of about six young five or six times a year. Within six weeks of birth the young are themselves capable of breeding. If each young mouse found a mate from outside his family and bred successfully, within one year a single pair could have tens of thousands of offspring. The same principle goes for all creatures: single plants may produce literally millions of pollen grains; single-celled creatures such as bacteria reproduce geometrically (2—4—8—16 and so on) many times a day. So why is the world not covered with mice, or with dandelions? Obviously, because they don't all survive; over-population necessarily means mortality.

Second is variation: within a species there is variability in bodily structure and function. Just look at man: even within the same family no two children are alike (except, of course, in the case of identical twins). There are differences in relatively trivial traits such as hair colour or fingerprints, but there are also important differences—differences which could influence survival—such as eyesight, or the ability to digest certain foods properly.

Third is inheritance: many features of an individual are passed on genetically to its offspring. In mice, coat colour is inherited; in man many abnormalities in digestion are inherited. In fact *most* characteristics are thought to be influenced by genetics to a greater or lesser extent.

If we put these three ingredients together we get a struggle for existence. Since the world cannot support infinite numbers of mice, or dandelions, or human beings for that matter, some will die and others will survive. Or, more subtly, some will survive with a little more success than others—may leave a few more offspring, for instance. This survival will depend in part upon the abilities of the creatures: a mouse possessing a trait which helped him to win a mate, or to fight for territory, or to hunt for food more efficiently than his competitors, will stand a greater chance of survival. Since many of these traits are inherited (or are at least influenced by inheritance), the mouse which survives better will contribute more young to the next generation than his less efficient competitor, and these young will automatically carry the genes which determined success. Over many generations the successful traits will therefore increase while the unsuccessful ones will die out and, given enough time, this will change a population in response to a changing environment, or to changing requirements for 'success'. That is natural selection, and neo-Darwinism maintains that such a process can lead to the origin of new species.

To envisage 'evolution in action', imagine a large population of bears living in North America before the arrival of man. If the bears were generally successful in their struggle for survival—if, for example, they encountered little competition from other species—they would probably spread out to occupy new areas. In this dispersal they would eventually encounter a variety of new food sources, competitors, climates and so on. If we think only of climate for a moment it is clear that a Rocky Mountain bear would find the Canadian Arctic rather cold, but southern California somewhat hot. If there was variability for traits such as fur thickness or fur colour then we might expect natural selection to favour different traits in different parts of the range; in other words we would expect some bears to survive better than others depending upon their ability to respond to changes in climate. So, given enough time, we would expect the bears in the far north to become different from those in the south—we would expect them to be larger (so as to conserve heat more efficiently) and to have a thick white coat (which is known to 'hold the warmth' more efficiently). Indeed, this is what is found in North America: the smaller brown Kodiak bear is found in the temperate Rocky Mountains while the larger white polar bear is restricted to the shores of the Arctic Ocean.

This is typical of the way in which neo-Darwinism can 'explain' many of the observations of nature (I say 'explain' in quotes because, convincing as the bear story is, such explanations are really *post-hoc* rationalizations rather than true, known, *reasons* for what is observed). In fact the North American bears fulfil yet more expectations of neo-Darwinism. Although the two bears—the Kodiak and the polar—are now geographically separate and are considered as separate species in taxonomy, they are capable of mating in captivity and of producing completely fertile offspring. This is just what we would expect if natural selection had acted relatively recently to adapt the bears to different environments. The neo-Darwinists would argue that, given enough time, these two *physically* disparate creatures will also become isolated *reproductively* to produce two true species. These bears are on the verge of speciation, the emergence of new species, and with the accumulation of only a few more differences they would no longer be capable of interbreeding.

Of course, neo-Darwinism admits that there are other means by which new species may arise. In many plants new mutants which are both physically *and* genetically 'new species' may appear in a single step, over one generation rather than thousands. In such cases the origin of species has nothing to do with the gradual accumulation of beneficial variants in response to the environment, it is rather an abrupt all-or-nothing event in which natural selection is reduced to a crude life-or-death role. Such dramatic events are the exception in neo-Darwinian theory; the bulk of new adaptations and new species are thought to arise gradually—the result of many changes over many generations.

The variability that selection can act upon is now known to reside largely in the genes. Mendel's crucial contribution to Darwinism was the discovery that many traits (such as the height, colour, or smoothness of peas and pea plants) are inherited from parents in little 'packages'. These packages are often either dominant (such as brown eyes in man) or recessive (blue eyes), although in the case of complex traits such as human height a sort of 'blending' inheritance is often seen (for instance, children are usually variable in height compared with their parents). Obviously if all the genes for eye colour were the same in human populations there would be no variability. The variation is due to random mutations, that is molecular 'mistakes' in the structure of the gene, which alter the effect of the gene on the creature. So 'blue' eye colour may have arisen as a mutant of 'brown' (or vice versa).

Most mutations are harmful because a random haphazard change in the functioning gene is more likely to be detrimental than beneficial. If you were to change the thread on a randomly chosen bolt on your car the result is more likely to be damaging than helpful because your car has already been designed to perform certain tasks in one way;

17

the random change is most likely to cause a breakdown. But, every so often, such a change might actually improve the performance of the car as a whole. It is these mutations that will determine differences in the 'performance' of creatures in nature, enabling natural selection to act upon them.

Darwin originally envisaged natural selection as a strong 'weeding-out' of the unfit by the environment. The neo-Darwinian synthesis sees selection not as an all-or-nothing power but more as a subtle influence which is really only detectable over many generations in large populations. This is not to say that selection acts 'for the good of the species'—this is a misconception of natural selection—just that it may be so subtle that it is only apparent in macrocosm. Take an example of a gene mutation which increases fertility by 1 per cent. If you were looking at shrimps you would be able to count the thousands of eggs which they produce and see that those having this gene each had 1 per cent more eggs. Yet if you were investigating elephants no such obvious difference would be seen; elephants don't have hundreds of young. Over *thousands* of generations, however, and in a large population, such a gene probably would be seen to spread slowly because every now and then the possession of such a gene could make the difference between reproductive success or failure.

Similarly, the different ways in which the environment can act to select features may be much more varied and subtle than was originally thought; the 'survival of the fittest' need not be the simple cliché of the antelope outrunning the leopard. Apart from such obvious environmental selection (by, say, climate or predators), selection can act on many aspects of day-to-day life:

1. Intra-specific competition, e.g. rivalry over territory between peers.
2. Inter-specific competition, e.g. rivalry between similar species over limited resources.
3. Sexual attraction, i.e. the ability to win a mate.
4. Fertility and fecundity, i.e. the physiological ability to bear maximum numbers of offspring.

2b

5. Parasites, i.e. susceptibility and resistance to internal or external parasites.

And many others.

Of course many of these aspects of life are interrelated, but they show the subtle and complex ways in which the 'survival of the fittest' can be manifested. Such complexity also makes it clear that selection is unlikely to act in simple, additive ways. It is unlikely, for instance, that a single gene mutation will only influence a single bodily trait. Since genes code for proteins and since proteins are the building blocks of life, involved in vastly complex biochemical pathways and chain reactions, the mutation of a single gene will almost certainly have a wide range of bodily 'symptoms'. Some of these symptoms may be beneficial but others are possibly harmful. So how does selection choose? This is a real difficulty in the conceptualization of natural selection, but one that is seen by the neo-Darwinists—at the moment, anyway—as a problem to be solved by further research rather than as a shortcoming of the theory itself.

This is the backbone of neo-Darwinism, the 'school textbook' version still taught in classrooms. As Theodosius Dobzhansky, one of the architects of the neo-Darwinian synthesis of the 1930s and 1940s, has said: 'Evolution is a change in the genetic composition of populations.' To the neo-Darwinists *then*, as to most now, this simple statement was seen as an adequate description of the basis of evolution. But there is now a strong, and growing, feeling that there is a lot more to evolution than genes alone.

Chapter 2

The problems begin . . .

———————————— ✹ ————————————

If *The Origin of Species* convinced *most* biologists that evolution had taken place by means of natural selection, the neo-Darwinian synthesis—which incorporated the laws of heredity into Darwinism—convinced the rest of them. Neo-Darwinism was such a formidable unifying principle from the 1930s onwards that virtually no respectable academic (in the English-speaking world at least) dared contradict it. Indeed, why should they? It is a convincing theory which at a stroke makes sense of the far-flung corners of the natural world: palaeontology and genetics, biogeography and taxonomy.

Ironically it is this apparent strength of the theory—that it can explain so much—which may be its Achilles' heel. Neo-Darwinism is incredibly ambitious; it attempts to explain a vast part of reality, all the subtlety and complexity of nature, in one breath. But do all the individual pieces of this cosmic jigsaw puzzle actually fit together? It is all very well to half close your eyes and imagine you see a coherent picture, but what is it like in close-up?

Because the theory is so ambitious one must expect flexibility within it to cope with the myriad specific cases posed by life on earth. Under conditions of extreme environmental stress, for example, one would expect natural selection to weed out unfit creatures much more effectively than in less taxing circumstances. So in order to be realistic the theory must not be dogmatic about the power of selection. That neo-Darwinism should be elastic enough to cope with a variety of observations is healthy and desirable. Nature *is* subtle and varied; any theory that explains nature must reflect these qualities.

The problems begin...

However, there is a real danger that in explaining so much the theory actually *explains* nothing. This is the core of the philosophical doubt facing Darwinism. An example of the perils of 'explaining too much' can be seen in the notion of adaptation. When a biologist finds a creature with an intricate and useful adaptation—such as the chameleon's ability to change colour to match its background—he immediately explains it in terms of natural selection and evolution. In fact the existence of such adaptations is frequently taken as proof of the power of selection. But what will the biologist say when he finds a similar lizard *without* this camouflage adaptation? The chances are he will conclude that such an adaptation is unnecessary for the survival of the second lizard, or that selection has not been strong enough to 'create' it. Both of these conclusions may be valid—they seem reasonable enough—but we are tempted now to ask him what sort of evidence would *contradict* the idea of selection? If the presence of adaptations is evidence *for* selection, but the absence of adaptations is not evidence *against* selection, then is it possible to deny the existence of selection at all? In other words if selection can explain everything then it really explains nothing. Good scientific theories should be testable and even falsifiable.

Another philosophical question regards the very definition of the word 'selection'. One of the original formulations of selection was 'the survival of the fittest'. If you open a standard textbook of genetics 'fitness' will probably be defined as 'the ability to survive' or something similar. But if the 'fittest' are defined as 'the best survivors' then the idea of natural selection becomes 'the survival of those best at surviving'. So what else is new? If there is no more to Darwinism than a truism then the whole theory rests on very shaky ground.

These philosophical doubts about the value of Darwinism and neo-Darwinism as science—is the theory falsifiable? Is it a tautology?—are not new; they have been expressed repeatedly since Darwin's time. But they are still in the air and some of the world's leading philosophers of science are still arguing over them. In Chapter 3 I take a look at these philosophical doubts facing Darwinism to see whether the theory meets the stringent requirements of 'good' science.

Among the biologists—as opposed to philosophers—there are doubts of different origin. What has caused concern scientifically is that when you look closely at the 'joins' in the jigsaw puzzle of evolutionary theory the individual pieces don't seem to interlock as neatly as it appeared they did from a distance. In Chapters 4 to 9 I investigate the six crucial areas of neo-Darwinism from which reassessment may come in the near future.

Is selection really so strong (Chapter 4)? If the philosophers are satisfied that the idea of selection is not tautologous, that it really is a useful scientific theory, our next task is to measure it in the wild and find out how powerful a force it is. This has posed some difficulties. Not only is natural selection extremely difficult to pin down and measure, but many of the observations of variation among plants and animals in different environments also appear to contradict the expectations of selection. Why is there so much variability in creatures in the first place? Why doesn't that variability respond to environmental stresses in any predictable way? The vast amount of genetic variation that is now known to exist in most species does not confer any obvious benefits. In addition, the variation doesn't occur as one would expect: species found in stable environments seem to show as much variability as species in changing, unstable environments, contrary to what Darwinian principles would lead one to expect.

How do new species arise (Chapter 5)? Darwin's original idea, that new species arise gradually from the action of natural selection over time, is now seriously in doubt. In fact Darwin was disappointingly vague and inexplicit about the actual mechanics of speciation (despite the title of his *magnum opus*). The events which lead to the 'creation' of new species are still largely a puzzle. Is selection alone strong enough to bring about new, distinct, sexually isolated species in the wild? Is this process necessarily a gradual one, or may new species arise quite abruptly? The results of thousands of experiments and observations from nature are ambiguous;

natural selection may be strong enough to create adaptations, but some recent experiments suggest that selection may actually be irrelevant in the origin of species. There is also a wrangle over the speed at which new species are formed—the latest results implying that this may be sudden rather than gradual.

Why don't we see gradual transition in the sequences of fossils (Chapter 6)? According to Darwin, and the current neo-Darwinists, the fossil record has gaps in it because of the haphazard way in which fossilization occurs—it is bound to be an imperfect record of the history of life. But is it? Is the jerky and abrupt nature of the record really just due to 'gaps', or does it reflect the way evolution actually happened? There is a strong feeling among leading palaeontologists that the punctuated history shown by fossils reflects the way life has evolved—in leaps and bounds rather than in gradual transition. There is also a growing sense that there is much more to understanding 'macroevolution'—the large-scale picture one gets from the fossils—than the simple idea of natural selection can alone explain.

Can we separate 'pattern' from 'process' (Chapter 7)? Every taxonomist since Darwin has interpreted life as a vast tree in which all living creatures are the tips of the branches, and fossils are the remains of ancestral branches. So the *pattern* of nature—the forms that exist now and in the past—has been interpreted in terms of the *process* of nature, the theory of branching evolution through time. But has this assumption clouded our vision of nature? Can we be certain that a particular fossil, which may appear to be intermediate between other creatures, is really an ancestor? With the growing sophistication of taxonomy there is a feeling that many of the neo-Darwinian assumptions about fossils and ancestry may be scientifically unfounded, and should be dropped. This realization, that the theory may be incapable of helping taxonomy, and may even be a hindrance to it, has led to a rejection of Darwinian ideas among some taxonomists who feel that we should be finding out more about the pattern before we become dogmatic about the process which is supposed to explain it.

Can genes learn from experience (Chapter 8)? Fifty years before Darwin published *The Origin of Species* the French naturalist Jean Baptiste de Lamarck had proposed a different theory of evolution. Instead of selection and variation as the driving force, Lamarck thought that creatures were actively capable of adapting to new circumstances and then passing this adaptation on to their offspring. This idea, that genes can 'learn from experience', lost favour after the publication of Darwin's theory, and is anathema to the neo-Darwinists because it denies the importance of random mutation and natural selection. Until recently there was little convincing evidence for Lamarckism and overwhelming evidence for neo-Darwinism. But recent research has thrown open the question again: a controversial series of experiments has tried to revive Lamarck's ideas. Even if these experiments prove unconvincing there are other results which suggest that the existing story is itself incomplete; inheritance certainly entails more than the simplistic laws that Mendel formulated.

Finally, can genes build bodies (Chapter 9)? One of the truly gaping holes in evolutionary theory is the void in our understanding of how genes actually construct bodies. This is important for neo-Darwinism because selection is usually thought to act on *individuals*, in terms of survival or fitness, and yet the central mathematical theory of natural selection is expounded in terms of *genes* (a distinction which, as we shall see, is crucial). Is there the implied simple one-to-one correspondence between genes and bodies? It would appear that there is not. The processes which cause a bag of genes to 'become' a multi-million-celled complex organism are still a huge mystery, but the most recent theories of development appear hard to reconcile with the mechanistic and 'reductionist' neo-Darwinism.

These are all questions over which biologists—who, in the past, would not have hesitated to call themselves Darwinists— are now deep in argument. In some cases the doubts have actually caused once-committed neo-Darwinists to reject the 'faith' and seek a new synthesis. Because science is notoriously 'blinkered', many workers are unaware that the doubts they may have about their own area of evolutionary theory are shared by others.

So who is right? Are the attacks valid? Will Darwinism survive?

Chapter 3

Is Darwinism a scientific theory?

———————————— ❊ ————————————

I have come to the conclusion that Darwinism is not a testable
scientific theory, but a metaphysical research programme . . .
Karl Popper, 1974

Before one can begin to investigate a particular scientific
theory about the world, it is necessary to be certain that the
theory is genuinely scientific in the first place. In other words
it must be possible to carry out experiments which will either
support or contradict the theory so that one can find out
whether it is basically 'right' or 'wrong'. The reason that a
belief in God is not scientific is that such experiments simply
are not possible; to a Christian *all* observations are taken to
be evidence for a God, and therefore it is by definition
impossible to show scientifically that God exists. (That is not
to say, of course, that He does not exist, just that He is not
accessible through logic, or reason.)

That Darwinism is a scientific theory would at first appear
glaringly obvious. Is it not a hypothesis about the influence
of the environment upon creatures, which we can test
through experiment? Have not thousands of scientists spent
lifetimes trying to test and elaborate the theory? Surely to
suggest that it is not properly scientific is pedantic nonsense?

Unfortunately, the fact that scientists have devoted their
lives to the study of Darwinism does not automatically mean
that the theory is necessarily scientific. The alchemists in the
Middle Ages spent their time and energy trying to convert
base metals into gold and, of course, failed. We can now see
that the theories underlying the alchemists' efforts were
fundamentally mistaken, and although they would

undoubtedly have considered themselves 'scientists', we would hesitate today to call their experiments scientific.

The philosophical problem with Darwinism is that it actually explains too much, that it is difficult to falsify by experimentation. Once again this seems a nonsense: how can the ability to explain too much be a problem for a theory? Surely a good theory should be able to explain all the observations of nature? Nevertheless it is a real problem, and one that is appreciated not only by the philosophers of science but also by some of the biologists actively engaged in evolutionary research. The difficulty is that if a theory explains all observations it is in danger of being unfalsifiable in the same way that the existence of God is unfalsifiable. As one evolutionary geneticist, Richard Lewontin, puts it:

> For what good is a theory that is guaranteed by its internal logical structure to agree with all conceivable observations, irrespective of the real structure of the world? If scientists are going to use logically unbeatable theories about the world, they might as well give up natural science and take up religion.
>
> *Lewontin, 1974*

And, as the quotation at the start of the chapter shows, the leading twentieth-century philosopher of science, Karl Popper, is also worried about the scientific status of Darwinism.

> . . . it must be possible for an empirical scientific system to be refuted by experience.
>
> *Popper, 1959*

When a man who has been described by eminent scientists as 'incomparably the greatest philosopher of science that has ever been' (Sir Peter Medawar, talking of Popper) accuses Darwinism of being metaphysics rather than science, then there is a case to answer. What is it? In what way does Darwinism fall short as a scientific theory?

Popper's original criticism of Darwinism was that it was unfalsifiable. Darwin's theory of evolution is an attempt to explain a historical process; it tries to suggest how living creatures of the past have changed through time to give the present-day world of nature. According to Popper any theory of history is automatically unfalsifiable because it describes a 'one-off' event, something which is not repeatable. We have no way of going back sixty million years to test our ideas about how the dinosaurs became extinct; it was a unique event in history which is inaccessible through experimentation. If it is not accessible through experiments it cannot be scientific, said Popper.

In a purist sense this criticism is valid. We will never know for certain why the dinosaurs died out because we will never be able to re-create the same conditions to test a theory about that event. Yet to many scientists, and even to several other philosophers of science, it seems ridiculously idealistic and short-sighted to call Darwinism unscientific on these grounds. If the dividing line between science and metaphysics is to be drawn on the criterion of falsifiability, then cosmology—a major part of astronomy which investigates the history of the universe—is automatically fiction whereas astrology and phrenology (the nineteenth-century myth that bumps on the head hold the secrets to health and happiness) are science. They may be *false* science, but they are falsifiable and therefore scientific. Similarly, if theories of history are automatically unscientific, it would be impossible to *prove* that the world existed yesterday. Surely this is carrying the rigour of science to the point of absurdity?

To be fair to Popper he has recently revised his thoughts on this aspect of Darwinism and conceded that since the theory is *testable* in some respects it is scientific to that extent. Although it will never be possible to falsify a theory about dinosaur extinction, it *is* possible to test such a theory by seeing how well the available evidence fits the explanation. Obviously some explanations are going to accord with the evidence better than others. To that extent the theory is testable and is therefore scientific.

It is rather like a murder trial: you can never be 100 per cent certain that the man who is found guilty is really the murderer unless you actually saw the event take place. What you *can* do is gather as much evidence as possible: the butler had blood on his hands, the gun was found in the butler's coat, the butler was seen buying the gun the day before the murder, and so on. If the evidence all points to one explanation then it is reasonable to assume that the butler 'did it'. To refuse to find him guilty because one cannot be 100 per cent certain of his guilt would be, in this case, purist to the point of stupidity.

Darwin's theory of evolution, therefore, passes muster as science even though it is not, strictly speaking, falsifiable. The same applies to other historical theories: the 'Big Bang' theory of cosmology is scientific so long as you can test it against observations from astronomy and physics. The theory that there was a battle of Waterloo in 1815 is scientific in so far as it can be tested against documentary evidence. It would seem that only the less ambitious theories—ones that restrict themselves to present and future events—can be strictly scientific in the sense of being falsifiable.

The philosophers have another bone to pick with evolutionary theory, one that has haunted Darwinism for a hundred years: is the idea of natural selection a tautology? A tautology is the saying of something twice over in different words, and is therefore either a nonsense or a statement which is so self-evident as to be meaningless. The statement 'several bachelors who were not married were at the meeting' is nonsense because bachelors *are* unmarried, while the sentence implies that they are not.

Much of mathematics is tautologous because of the way in which the basic premises are defined. For example, the statement 'one plus one is two' is a tautology because of the very definitions of the words; it is totally inconceivable that 'one plus one' should give any other result than 'two'. The numbers and functions of addition or subtraction are defined such that no other result is possible. That is not to say that mathematics is useless. Within the rules and definitions it is a powerful tool for untangling the relations of numbers. The point is that it is not in a position to tell us anything *new* about the outside world. It is not testable against reality. No amount of investigation will change the fact that 'eight

29

divided by four is two' because the result is a logical restatement of the initial conditions. For a scientific statement to avoid being tautologous, therefore, it must propose some relationship in the world that is testable by experiment.

The problem of tautology in Darwinism is a subtle one. It hinges on the definitions of a few crucial words: 'the survival of the fittest.' This is the central claim that Darwin made, that only the 'fittest' succeed in a struggle for 'survival'. If this basic statement does not tell us anything new about the outside world then the whole of Darwinism is in deep trouble. Unfortunately the senses in which these words are often used by biologists do turn the statement into a nonsense.

If you turn to a textbook of genetics in search of a definition of 'fitness' you will find something like this:

> The genotype with the largest survival rate is defined as the fittest . . .
>
> *Goodenough and Levine, 1975*

So the central statement of Darwinism, 'the survival of the fittest', becomes: 'the survival of those creatures having the largest survival rate'! Immediately the problem is clear; if you define fitness as 'the ability to survive' then the 'survival of the fittest' becomes a tautology, a self-evident bit of trivia. In this form the statement doesn't tell us anything about the outside world that we didn't know already. It doesn't, for example, enable us to predict which members of a population will survive and reproduce, since we cannot measure survival until *afterwards.* In this sense the neo-Darwinists must avoid a sloppy attitude to their theory or it will turn out to say nothing.

Yet the basic idea of natural selection need not necessarily be tautologous; it can be seen to propose a relationship which is testable. There obviously *is* a vast over-production of life in relation to the available resources; and the idea that survival is non-random is definitely *testable*. What is needed for a meaningful theory is a different definition of fitness. If one can suggest *why* a creature might survive, in terms of its structure or functions, in a given environment better than

30

another creature then the 'survival of the fittest' becomes meaningful again.

Take the polar bears of the Arctic as an example. If you could show that there is over-production, that more bears are born than can survive; and if you could show *why* the survivors do survive, if you could suggest, for instance, which features (such as the ability of the fur to retain warmth) the survivors have in common, then you would be in a position to make a meaningful scientific statement about natural selection. You could predict, for example, that 'only those bears having a thick coat will survive the cold Arctic winter'. Such a statement is testable by experiment, and therefore not tautologous. (This is not to say that such an apparently reasonable statement is *correct*; as we shall see in later chapters, there are profound problems in trying to show the validity of even the most basic Darwinian ideas.)

In both of these philosophical senses, Darwinism can stand up as good science. Although it is not strictly falsifiable, it is certainly, in principle, a testable theory. Similarly, although by some definitions of the word 'fitness' the idea of 'survival of the fittest' becomes a self-evident statement, it is possible to define fitness (recognizing the interaction of a creature with its environment) in such a way that natural selection is a predictive, non-tautological, theory.

There is one final argument that philosophers have with Darwinism which is not specifically aimed at evolutionary theory. It is, rather, a general criticism of many scientific theories. This is the problem of reductionism.

In some ways reductionism is an essential part of science because it is a belief—almost a faith—that by analysing in greater and greater depth a *part* of a system we will come to understand the whole system better, that by finding out the rules at one level in nature we will be able eventually to 'join up' all the levels. Twenty or thirty years ago—and in some cases even more recently—reductionism was all the rage. There was a sense of confidence, even arrogance, in science that ultimately all the levels of scientific knowledge would be joined together so that biology would be explained in terms of biochemistry; biochemistry in terms of chemistry;

chemistry in terms of physics, and so on. Reductionists believed that, given enough time, we should be able to understand the most complex human behaviour in terms of subatomic physics.

Darwinism is implicitly a reductionist theory because it suggests that observations at many different levels of nature—from the mass extinction of creatures over millions of years to the submicroscopic event called mutation—may all be explained by reference to a single, unifying principle: natural selection. The events of the fossil record are seen as the result, on a large scale, of individual competition; and the changes in gene frequencies which are seen as the underlying basis of evolution are the result, on a small scale, of the same thing—individual competition and survival.

The philosophers are not in a position to say that this is wrong, or that reductionism in general is mistaken, but there is a definite swing away from this all-embracing view of science. There is a growing feeling that perhaps we are actually missing something by this approach, that it is rather naïve and simplistic. A good example can be seen in the study of animal behaviour. In the 1950s and 1960s the study of behaviour was widely considered to be 'soft' science, science that lacked the rigour and exactitude of, say, physics because it had somehow 'jumped the gun'. How could you possibly understand the social interactions of animals properly before you understood the brain, and biochemistry? Since the root of all social behaviour was in the workings of individual brains, there was surely no point in trying to develop the science of behaviour until neurophysiology and neuroanatomy were understood. Now, of course, we realize that there are complex patterns in behaviour and social interaction which deserve research but which are in no way derivable from our understanding of the brain or of biochemistry. In other words it is possible to make original statements about behaviour without any understanding of brain function. Similarly we cannot rely on neurophysiologists to predict the findings of behaviour; animal behaviour today is a popular and expanding field of science yielding insights which are inaccessible through more 'basic' routes.

Is Darwinism a scientific theory?

Nature seems to be analysable at various levels—atoms, molecules, cells, individuals, societies—and the rules underlying events at each of these levels are not necessarily related to the rules at other levels. If we assume that the most complex of events are ultimately explicable in terms of electrons and protons we are quite likely to miss much of the subtlety of nature. Nature is a hierarchy of complexity, and perhaps we should be wary of theories which try to embrace too much too soon.

This unease with the reductionism of Darwinian theory is detectable in several places. The most obvious is probably sociobiology, in which it has become fashionable—among some sociobiologists at least—to try to explain social behaviour in animals in terms of single genes, such as 'selfish' or 'altruistic' genes (see also Chapter 4, p. 57-8). Many biologists are sceptical of the simplistic assumptions underlying such potentially controversial science. Another sensitive area at the moment is palaeontology. Many—perhaps most—palaeontologists are beginning to feel quite strongly that there is a great deal more to the fossil record than can be predicted by natural selection alone. In a recent research textbook (*Patterns of Evolution*, edited by Hallam, 1977), for example, eleven out of fifteen of the world's leading palaeontologists expressed doubts about the conventional 'gradualist' interpretation of the fossil record—an interpretation by which Darwin himself set much store. This gradualism was originally derived from an impression of the way in which natural selection acts; since selection was thought to act slowly to produce adaptation it was assumed that the fossils themselves would show gradual change over time. But, as modern palaeontologists now recognize, there is no such obvious trend in the fossils. The fossil record, they argue, is open to a different interpretation in which creatures change quite rapidly and then remain unchanged for great lengths of time. Once again the 'reductionist' expectation—that events at the 'macro' level should be directly derivable from an appreciation of the 'micro' level—has foundered.

It is not that these observations may actually contradict

33

Darwinism, it is more that the simple principle of natural selection seems inadequate to understand and predict all the phenomena of evolution. Perhaps evolution entails more than the simple 'differential survival of genes', and it is this feeling that underlies the current sense of dissatisfaction with reductionism.

Finally, we cannot leave any philosophical argument about Darwinism without mentioning what is undoubtedly the single most controversial and 'live' aspect of the whole subject today: creationism. It is a telling indicator of the power held by the creationist lobby in the United States that the American President felt it necessary to say, of evolutionary theory:

> Well, it is a theory, it is a scientific theory only, and it has in recent years been challenged in the world of science and is not yet believed in the scientific community to be as infallible as it once was believed. But if it was going to be taught in the schools, then I think that also the biblical theory of creation, which is not a theory but the biblical story of creation, should also be taught.
>
> *Ronald Reagan, 1980*

Because evolution is one explanation of how life has come to be as it is, it is a 'world-view'—almost a philosophy. Although biologists are now arguing about *how* evolution has taken place, about whether Darwinian ideas are adequate to explain evolution, no more than a tiny fraction of them would actually deny the basic idea of evolution itself. No informed scientist could deny that life has existed for hundreds of millions of years, and that species have appeared and disappeared over that time. In fact there appear to be only two alternatives to evolution as explanations for nature: steady state theory, and creationism.

'Steady state' biology proposes that evolution has not actually taken place at all, but that all existing species have *always* existed. This assumes both that the earth has always existed and that conditions on earth have always been more or less as they are today. The trouble with this idea is that you can hardly deny extinction—there are no dinosaurs

34

romping around today—so steady state theory must really be 'degeneration' theory, which poses all sorts of other difficulties. Degeneration implies that the number of species is continually being eroded by extinction; but then where did all the species come from to begin with? And where are the Pre-Cambrian (700 million year-old) remains of, say, man? Despite uncertainties about the age of the earth and about the sequences of fossils, there is simply no reason to think that 'things have always been as they are now'. In terms of existing observations, steady state theory is a non-starter.

What about creationism, which is enjoying such a revival in the United States? Is there any reason to take seriously the notion of 'scientific creationism' as it is now called? This is an important and timely question because of the recent court battles in Arkansas and Louisiana over the 'Balanced Treatment' bills which have attempted to force school biology teachers to present both evolution and creation as equally valid theories of life. (Which is not to suggest that Bible-based religion and evolution are mutually exclusive faiths. The official Christian churches accept evolution in principle but maintain that the origin of life and the 'guiding hand' of evolution remain in God's power, an opinion which is shared by a surprisingly large number of 'good neo-Darwinists'. When I refer here to creationists I mean the extremists, those who adopt a literal interpretation of Genesis.)

It is actually very difficult to take seriously many of the creationists because of the blatantly unscientific nature of their approach.

> It is high time that Christians face the fact that the so-called geologic ages are essentially synonymous with the evolutionary theory of origins. The latter, in turn, is at its ultimate roots the anti-God conspiracy of Satan himself.
>
> *Henry Morris, 1978*

Presumably what Morris (who, incidentally, is Director of the Institute for Creation Research in San Diego) means is that fossils were planted by Satan to confuse us.

Is there any *scientific* reason put forward by the creationists that would make us reject evolution in favour of creation?

The prime tenet of creationism, according to Morris, is that 'the physical universe of space, time, matter and energy has not always existed, but was supernaturally created by a transcendent personal creator who alone has existed from eternity'. So, from the start, the creationists admit that their theory is 'supernaturual', that it is inaccessible by logic and science. Since, by definition, a supernatural phenomenon cannot be proved scientifically, there can be no evidence for creation, only evidence against evolution.

This is the essence of the creationist argument: an uneasy combination of faith in creation combined with evidence against evolution. And clearly there *are* several areas of evolution that are incomplete and many difficulties in the theory. Setting aside the really ridiculous claims (one, for example, that a shod human footprint has been found in Cambrian rock along with some crushed trilobites (about 650 million years ago)), what are the most serious attacks on evolution that the creationists can muster?

The oldest problem with evolution, and the one that creationists still rely upon, is the difficulty of explaining intermediate forms in the development of complex adaptations such as the eye, or wings, etc. Such difficulties are real—I don't think there is an evolutionist alive who is particularly happy with existing ideas about how complex features arise. Darwin himself confessed that to imagine the eye as having evolved by selection was almost absurd—could all the nerves and muscles and bone sockets really arise through random variation and selection alone? Another problem concerns the power of natural selection itself: it may be able to change populations, but can it cause the origin of totally new species? This is another question that has stretched the minds of Darwinists. Yet for all its faults and weaknesses there is an important distinction between Darwinism and creationism: Darwinism is a rigorous scientific attempt to *explain* what we see in nature. Just because there are difficulties in it one should not abandon reason and resort to blind faith or 'the hand of God'. After all, examples abound of natural phenomena—such as lightning—which, because they were not understood, were once considered proof of 'the hand of God'. Is it not the hallmark of a mature society to seek explanation rather than hide behind mythology?

Perhaps the commonest criticism of evolution—or, more accurately, of Darwinism—made by creationists concerns the role of chance in evolution. How, they ask, can a series of chance, or random, events—mutations—give rise to the integrated complexity and order that we see around us? Reasonable as this comment sounds, it betrays a misunderstanding of the role of chance in evolutionary theory. The creationists make an analogy with bricks and ask: 'Do you expect me to believe that it is possible to throw a huge pile of bricks together so that they will fall into place as a house?' An unlikely event to be sure. But the analogy is mistaken. Although individual bricks—genes—*do* get thrown together by chance, they don't all get thrown together *at once*. The proper analogy would be to ask: 'Do you expect me to believe that it is possible for a single brick to be thrown into an existing house, and for it sometimes to land in a useful position?' I think everyone would have to admit the possibility of that. In other words the chance element is there, since single genes do mutate at random, but it plays a much smaller role than the creationists believe. The answer to the second question may still be 'pretty unlikely', but it is a lot more likely than the first.

Some of the more informed creationists have certainly exploited the chinks in the neo-Darwinian armour with subtlety. They point to the difficulties now facing some parts of the theory, in particular the philosophical questions as to whether Darwinism is science at all; then, rather than trying to show that creationism deserves equal time as science, they turn the whole problem around and claim that since Darwinism is so shaky *both* theories are really metaphysical and therefore deserve equal time! (One wonders how such creationists would react to a demand that evolution be given equal time at religious meetings.)

Of course Darwinism, and evolution, have flaws. But evidence *against* evolution is certainly not evidence *for*

37

creation. Creationism has no scientific argument with evolution. For all its flaws evolution is science, whereas creationism is based upon faith. That creationism has, in some parts of the United States, achieved equal time in school biology is a travesty of education because science doesn't work on the principle of *fairness*, or equal time, it works on the principle of *merit*. Creationism has no scientific merit; if you want proof of that just try asking a creationist if he can envisage falsification of his ideas through experiment.

Chapter 4

How strong is natural selection?

———————————— ✸ ————————————

So far as we now know, not only is natural selection inevitable, not only is it *an* effective agency of evolution, but it is *the* only effective agency of evolution.

Julian Huxley, 1953

To the present moment no one has succeeded in measuring with any accuracy the net fitnesses of genotypes for any locus, in any species, in any environment, in nature.

Richard Lewontin, 1974

Once it had been established that evolution had taken place, attention was inevitably turned to the question of *how* it had occurred. Darwin's driving force for evolution, natural selection, has been under close scrutiny ever since (especially over the last twenty-five years) and for over a century evolutionary thought has been dominated by the argument as to whether natural selection exists at all, and—if it does exist—whether it is powerful enough to create adaptations and new species. This, in a sense, is the original attack on Darwinism that was quelled by the modern synthesis of the 1930s and 1940s but which, in several guises, has returned of late with a renewed vigour. Today, there are strong doubts about where selection can act (does it act on groups, or on individuals, or on the level of the 'selfish' gene?); there are doubts as to whether selection can create new species; and there are even doubts that selection can account for the basic adaptations of creatures.

Opinion about the strength of natural selection has varied enormously among even the most ardent Darwinists and neo-

Darwinists. Darwin himself was typically undogmatic in his original formulation:

> Can we doubt (remembering that many more individuals are born than can possibly survive) that individuals having any advantage, however slight, over others, would have the best chance of surviving and procreating their kind?
>
> *Darwin, 1859*

He believed that selection was '. . . the main, but not the exclusive means of' change and he seems to have been aware that hard evidence for selection in nature was difficult to pin down. On the other hand Alfred Russel Wallace, the co-discoverer of the idea of evolution by means of selection, was rather more Darwinian than Darwin himself and believed that natural selection was the exclusive power behind all observable traits in creatures. Not every biologist was so enamoured with the principle of selection. Even in Darwin's lifetime there were several dark clouds hanging over his theory.

The opening chapter of *The Origin of Species* was entitled 'Variation under Domestication' and is devoted to showing how artificial breeding by man can give rise to a remarkable diversity among some plants and animals. One need only imagine the various breeds of dog to see the range of variation that lies potentially in a single species of creature, and how to bring out that hidden variability: selective breeding (see fig. 1). In domestic breeding only those creatures with the desired trait are bred from. In relatively few generations this can give rise to specialized stocks showing highly exaggerated features, often bearing little resemblance to the parent stock.

Darwin drew the comparison between man and nature and suggested that if, through competition or environmental stresses, some variants of the same species survived better than others, would not nature act as a breeder to mould and shape populations? The variation was certainly there—Darwin could see that most species show variability in their characteristics whether this be anatomical, behavioural, or physiological. The struggle for survival was also obvious.

Fig. 1. The extent of the variability that may lie hidden in a wild creature is surprising. In a few thousand years the ancestral wild dog has been bred selectively to yield diverse breeds.

Was it not reasonable to assume, therefore, that the differential survival of creatures in the wild was a sort of global breeding programme acting to select and create new varieties? Expressed in these terms natural selection sounds not only reasonable, it sounds inevitable.

Despite the intuitive appeal and apparent inevitability of natural selection, a concrete demonstration of its power has proved elusive. There are few convincing cases where selection appears to have acted, in the wild, to change a population. Even among the convincing examples, such as the melanic moths of industrial Britain, there is no sign that a new species has ever been created through selection. To show that selection is a valid explanation for the origin of species, or even that it is a valuable scientific tool for evolutionists, has proved virtually impossible.

Before looking at natural selection itself, we must ask whether the analogy between artificial and natural selection is a useful one. Artificial selection is largely an all-or-nothing process in which the undesirable creatures make *no* contribution to breeding. This inevitably leads to a loss of variability through increased inbreeding, and inbreeding is known to cause severe problems of malformation and infertility. We have only to consider the social taboo in man against cousin marriages to realize that inbreeding is known to cause problems rather than 'bring out the best' in a family. Although we may see the successes of artificial breeding in rose gardens or meat markets, what we don't see are the many failures and the difficulties.

> . . . although quite rapid change can be produced in a population by artificial selection, the changes are often limited in extent and are associated with a general lowering of fitness. In so far as this is true, it is discouraging to any attempt to explain evolution as the result of selection.
>
> *Maynard Smith, 1966*

This is a significant admission from Britain's leading evolutionist. The 'limited' changes refer to the fact that under artificial selection one usually sees a fairly rapid shift in the desired characters, but after a few generations the responsiveness 'runs dry' and no more change is seen. Since visible variation is simply a reflection of gene variation and since genes are thought to mutate to form new variants relatively infrequently, this running dry is hardly surprising. There cannot be a bottomless well of new variants over a short time span. Nevertheless this does demonstrate the limits on the power of a breeder to change the breed.

A final, but important cautionary note to artificial selection is that when an artificial breed is 'returned to the wild'—allowed to breed with a wild creature—almost immediately (within only a few generations) the offspring revert back to the original form. This suggests that selection in the wild could cause significant changes to a population only if the environmental stresses were strong (to mimic, say, artificial selection), or if there was isolation of the population to avoid interbreeding with 'wild', unselected, creatures.

How could we demonstrate convincingly that natural

selection is capable of changing a population's characteristics in the wild? According to Richard Lewontin, one of America's leading evolutionary geneticists, the most convincing way to demonstrate selection would be to study, say, one hundred randomly chosen examples of inherited variations in creatures and attempt to pin down the environmental forces which bestow advantages or disadvantages upon these variants. If in the majority of cases it is possible to show convincingly that the environment is determining the increase, or decrease, in variants, we would have good reason to believe that natural selection can bring about adaptation. It is precisely this task that population geneticists (geneticists who study heredity in groups of interbreeding creatures) have been concentrating on for most of the past twenty-five years. From counting bands on snails to bristle hairs on fruit flies, population geneticists have been devoted to demonstrating the ways in which selection can—or cannot—mould species to their environments.

Take an example from man: hair colour. Suppose we knew that hair colour was genetically determined and that there was variability for this trait (both of which are actually true), might we not expect selection to act upon hair colour? If we could now show that in every human population redheads were more frequent where there was, say, high rainfall, or a colder climate, then we would have good *prima facie* evidence that natural selection had given rise to this distribution—in other words that red hair is an adaptation to high rainfall or to cold weather. We would then be interested to find out *why* red hair should bestow this advantage, but in the meantime selection would look a safe bet as the cause of the distribution. If we could do the same for a hundred randomly chosen types of variation—say, eye colour, or height, or whatever—then the evidence for selection would look convincing.

However, the results of such efforts have been rather ambiguous. There are a few successes: the research on mimicry in butterflies and moths clearly shows that there are definite advantages bestowed on individuals mimicking distasteful species. And there are some notable failures: in the most widely studied species of all—man—there is little evidence for *any* selective advantage or disadvantage for most of the dozens of the human blood-group types. The overall impression is one of confusion.

One creature that has received a great deal of attention in the study of selection is the common European land snail *Cepaea nemoralis*. This snail is variable in shell colour (pink, yellow, or brown) and in shell banding (the shell can have from nought to five dark bands wound around it). It is widespread through Europe and virtually every population of the snail is variable for these traits. So the obvious question is: why the variability? Does selection act on the snail's shell? Are certain types of colour or banding pattern more frequent in some habitats? Dozens of population geneticists have devoted a total of hundreds of academic man-years to investigating the *Cepaea* snails; yet the range of opinion as to which selective forces, if any, influence the snails' shells is more varied today than it was thirty years ago. There have been convincing demonstrations of localized climatic selection (yellow shells, for example, often appear more frequently in warmer habitats), of visual predation (thrushes appear to predate *Cepaea* shells selectively according to the cryptic properties the shell bestows), and of random variation (some *Cepaea* populations appear to vary in the chaotic manner one would expect if the genes 'drift' through populations, without any selection at all). But no single factor has been shown to influence the snail's shell in a consistent, predictable, way.

Even if one investigates the fairly *convincing* examples of selection in snails, the task of isolating the actual selective force can be very elusive. If one finds an excess of yellow snails in warmer habitats what can one conclude? What is it in the environment that is selecting yellow—is it insolation (the sun's direct light), or maximum temperature, or lack of frost, or perhaps lower rainfall, or even a combination of all these? What is it about yellow that it survives better in the warmer habitats—is it a direct property bestowed by the snail's shell colour, or is it a related physiological difference that just happens to be genetically associated with yellow? In the case of both the environment and the genetics there are extremely complex interactions which make any attempt at analysis virtually impossible. Just as you cannot 'hold everything else constant' when looking at the effect of temperature in a habitat, so you cannot study the isolated influence of a single gene in an intricately balanced set of genes that makes up a creature. Besides, the chances are that if some aspect of a creature is important for survival—such as agility for a lion, or cold adaptation for a polar bear—then it is unlikely to be drastically changed by single genes. Such characteristics are much more likely to show continuous, multi-gene variation because they involve the close interaction of so many different physiological and anatomical factors.

In order to study selection, geneticists have looked at gene frequency changes in populations; but selection, if it acts at all, must act on the 'myriad and subtle changes in size, shape, behaviour, and interactions with other species that constitute the real stuff of evolution' (Lewontin, 1974). This is not to say that selection doesn't act; just that it is surprisingly difficult to pin down.

What we can measure is by definition uninteresting and what we are interested in is by definition immeasurable.

Lewontin, 1974

Let us look at another classic example of supposed selection to show the difficulty. The peppered moth *Biston betularia* has a normal pale, speckled form and a melanic form. The melanic form was unknown in the early nineteenth century and gradually spread through the industrialized areas of northern England from about 1850 to the present day. The moth is eaten by birds which feed during the day when the moths are sitting on tree trunks. In the industrial areas the tree trunks became blackened by soot and this meant that the melanic moths on the trees were well camouflaged whereas the pale ones were more noticeable. It can be shown experimentally that birds can be fooled by this camouflage and will notice the pale-on-soot moths more easily than the melanic-on-soot moths. Surely it is reasonable to assume, therefore, that the spread of the melanic gene has been due to natural selection bestowing an advantage in the industrial areas of northern England?

It may be reasonable to assume this but it is not, in fact, scientific. It turns out, for example, that the melanic moths may also have a physiological advantage over the normal ones—more melanic moth eggs survive under normal conditions than do 'pale' eggs. Even in the absence of birds, therefore, one would expect such a gene (causing both melanism *and* increased egg production) to spread through a population rapidly. We now have two separate selective forces to consider—colour and egg production. It is still possible to argue that the melanics have spread because of a colour advantage (rather than an egg-production advantage), but we would also have to argue that the normal forms are maintained elsewhere—i.e. in non-industrial Britain—*despite* an egg-production disadvantage. And then, even if we could do that, are we sure (and this is the crucial point) that such a gradual change in gene frequency could ultimately lead to the splitting of a parent population into new species? If so, why haven't they done so already? The difficulties of demonstrating natural selection are hard enough; to demonstrate that a gene frequency change can also lead to species-formation is ten times harder still. One can begin to see how the apparently 'obvious' notion of selection can turn into an impossibly complex question when close analysis is attempted.

Over the past ten years or so some population geneticists have taken a different approach to the problem of demonstrating the power of selection. The knowledge of genetics, they argue, together with the theoretical understanding of how selection *may* act, should enable predictions to be made about the genetics of populations. If such general predictions hold good, then surely we have further evidence for selection?

1. How much genetic variability is there? Since gene mutations are thought to be infrequent, then if selection is very strong we would expect to find relatively little variability, since much 'weeding out' will have occurred.

2. Do alternative gene variants bestow definite advantages or disadvantages on the bearer? Once again, if selection is strong we would expect *small* gene changes to be important for survival.

3. Do species that have remained the same for millions of years—such as the cockroach—have less genetic variability than rapidly evolving ones? We would expect so; after all, such creatures are presumably 'locked in' to a stable way of life, and would lose unnecessary gene variants through 'stabilizing' selection.

4. Do creatures from very stable environments, such as the depths of the sea, show less genetic variability than ones from transient, or varied environments? Once again, we would expect this to be so if selection is strong. A varied environment should be able to support a variable population, whereas we would expect a restrictive environment to 'weed out' variation more vigorously.

In fact, considering the hundreds of species which have been studied in thousands of investigations, there are very few cases in which these four major expectations of selection theory have been fulfilled by the findings of genetics. The great flurry of activity in population genetics over the past twenty years has proved fruitless in terms of the old expectations.

The first big surprise has been the discovery of large amounts of genetic variability. Something like one in ten of all the body's genes have alternatives existing within any one creature. For non-critical traits, such as eye colour in man, or the number of stripes on a zebra, this may not be surprising. But the great majority of genes produce proteins that are part of highly complex biochemical cycles and pathways essential for survival. Such vast amounts of variability have surprised and puzzled geneticists: why is it there? How is it maintained? What is perhaps even more surprising is that these alternatives do not usually appear to differ from one another in terms of bestowing significant advantages or disadvantages on the creature. Although the variation is real, the selection does not seem crucial. It is as if, just as eye colour seems

47

irrelevant to human survival, so all the various biochemical processes within the body have many interchangeable parts— different varieties of components performing the same tasks with no apparent advantages or disadvantages associated with most of them. And *that* implies that selection is not weeding out the variants with any particular fervour.

Similarly, stable habitats or environments do not appear to contain less variable creatures. Deep-sea fish, which presumably experience an extremely monotonous environment (high pressure, no light, restricted diet), have just as much genetic variability as the nimble fruit fly *Drosophila*. So also, creatures 'from the past', such as the coelocanth or the cockroach, which appear to have remained physically the same for tens of millions of years, do not have lower genetic variability than the others. What do they need such variations for? How and why is it maintained if it is never used?

Population genetics—which is at the very heart of Darwinism—appears to be in the midst of a crisis of confidence over its inability to demonstrate selection convincingly and its relative ignorance about whether selection could actually lead to the 'origin of species'. The elaborate theoretical framework built up during the 'synthesis' days of the 1930s and 1940s has not matched the observations of reality. Lewontin has expressed the problem almost poetically:

> For many years population genetics was an immensely rich and powerful theory with virtually no suitable facts on which to operate. It was like a complex and exquisite machine, designed to process a raw material that no one had succeeded in mining. Occasionally some unusually clever or lucky prospector would come upon a natural outcrop of high-grade ore, and part of the machinery would be started up to prove to its backers that it really would work. But for the most part the machine was left to the engineers, forever tinkering, forever making improvements, in anticipation of the day when it would be called upon to carry out full production.

Quite suddenly the situation has changed. The mother-lode has been tapped and facts in profusion have been poured into the hoppers of this theory machine. And from the other end has issued—nothing. It is not that the machinery does not work, for a great clashing of gears is clearly audible, if not deafening, but it somehow cannot transform into a finished product the great volume of raw material that has been provided. The entire relationship between the theory and the facts needs to be reconsidered.

Lewontin, 1974

Although he is one of the leading American population geneticists, Lewontin's opinions are not shared by all neo-Darwinists. There is still a strong 'pro-selectionist' tradition flourishing in British population genetics, and in some North American circles. This is partly because there is a convincing history of demonstrating artificial selection in laboratory conditions. The fruit fly *Drosophila* has been bombarded with artificial selective pressures for countless aspects of its anatomy and physiology, and has responded convincingly to virtually all these pressures. Why, many would argue, should this not happen in the wild? To such scientists the idea of rejecting selection as the shaping force of evolution seems extreme and unhelpful—is there, they might ask, something better to put in its place?

Yet it has become a widely held view, particularly among certain American and Japanese geneticists, that much of the variation serves little purpose in the survival of creatures, and that it may represent neutral 'noise' in the system. This is not necessarily to deny that selection exists, nor that selection can cause adaptation, but to emphasize that selection may be a much weaker force than has previously been thought, and that a large proportion of the genetic variability observed in nature may serve no useful function. Motoo Kimura is a Japanese population geneticist and the most ardent proponent of this 'neutralism'. For Kimura, the majority of genetic variants are neutral in their effect, bestowing neither advantage nor disadvantage on the bearer and capable of drifting through populations unhindered by selection. Variation arises by mutation and may survive because it causes no harm. Kimura certainly has little time for those

49

who see selection as the omnipotent force in evolution, the 'naïve pan-selectionists'.

> The picture of evolutionary change that actually emerged from molecular studies seemed to me to be quite incompatible with the expectations of neo-Darwinism.
>
> *Kimura, 1977*

One of the findings of molecular studies that Kimura is referring to, and that has helped to shape his ideas, is the so-called molecular clock. If one looks at the molecular structure of certain complex organic compounds (such as the pigments haemoglobin or cytochrome) which are virtually ubiquitous in the plant and animal worlds, one can count the molecular differences between different species. Man's cytochrome, for example, may differ from that of a horse by ten molecular differences, presumably due to the accumulation of ten gene mutations since the two lineages split. The curious discovery was made some ten to fifteen years ago that these molecular differences appear to accumulate in a regular way so that the greater the time since divergence of a lineage (as told from the fossil record) the greater the number of molecular differences. This is as one might expect, except that the regularity is very striking; there is a virtual straight-line correspondence between molecular differences and time since divergence (see fig. 2).

This striking correlation strongly suggests one thing: that gene mutations are occurring regularly and that as they crop up they are being incorporated into the body chemistry almost automatically. This also implies that selection is not acting to 'weed out' such mutants, in other words that the vast majority of mutations are neutral in their effects. Kimura regards the molecular clock as strong evidence in support of his neutralist theory. So it is, except that the data from the molecular clock studies must be viewed with some scepticism. The fossil record is notoriously unreliable when it comes to estimates of age and divergence; similarly, the molecular differences require confirmation from many independent molecules. Not all compounds show the cytochrome 'clockwork' changes.

How strong is natural selection?

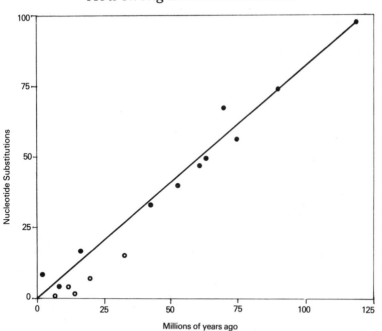

Fig. 2. Estimated nucleotide substitutions observed in seven proteins in 16 pairs of mammals, plotted against the time since members of each pair diverged. Except for primates (open circles) the points fall close to a straight line. (After Fitch)

The 'pan-selectionism' of the neo-Darwinists and the neutralism of Kimura and his supporters represent two extremes of interpretation regarding natural selection. To Kimura genes drift through populations as they arise and are generally of little use to the bearer. To the staunch neo-Darwinists drift is virtually a dirty word:

> I consider it . . . exceedingly unlikely that any gene will remain selectively neutral for any length of time.
>
> *Mayr, 1963*

Despite the failure of population genetics to predict or even explain observations, the neo-Darwinist position remains popular; there is probably not one British population geneticist who would openly agree with Lewontin's cynicism or with Kimura's rejection of neo-Darwinism. This is partly because of the strong evidence from experimental selection research (such as the *Drosophila* work mentioned earlier). It is also due to the single most important feature of all biology: *adaptation*.

How can you deny natural selection when the fact of adaptation is staring you in the face? A bird flies because it has wings; if the wings don't function properly, the bird will die. The bird is adapted to flight, and any alteration in its ability to fly will alter this adaptation. And, since genetic mutations must play a direct role in adaptation, natural selection must exist. So why all the difficulties in demonstrating it?

Several biologists have tried to reconcile the awkward contradictions posed by adaptation, by apparent neutralism, and by the difficulties of demonstrating natural selection. This is a very exciting area of biology because it appears to be at a stage where it is not new data that are necessary, just a new way of looking at the old data. A heuristic jump is in the offing.

Stephen Jay Gould and Richard Lewontin have proposed an interesting and entertaining way of looking at adaptations, and thinking about the importance of selection in evolution. Look at a Gothic building, they say, such as King's College Chapel, Cambridge, with a view to function and design. To the uninitiated eye the spandrels at the centres of the ceiling vaults, which bear beautiful designs in the chapel, will appear functional. They appear to serve a purpose. In fact the spandrel has no function whatever; it is an inevitable concomitant of the fact that when two Gothic arches meet, an inverted triangle *must* result. Once the architectural constraints are understood, the spandrel is seen for what it is: an unavoidable consequence. If the spandrel has to be there, why not paint it ornamentally to enhance the beauty of the building? The arch has a function; the spandrel simply exists because of the arch (see fig. 3).

Gould and Lewontin draw the analogy with organic structure. Why do we insist on seeing every feature of every creature as if it must have a function, a purpose? Perhaps there are organic 'spandrels'—biological features which simply exist because of other, functional aspects. An example

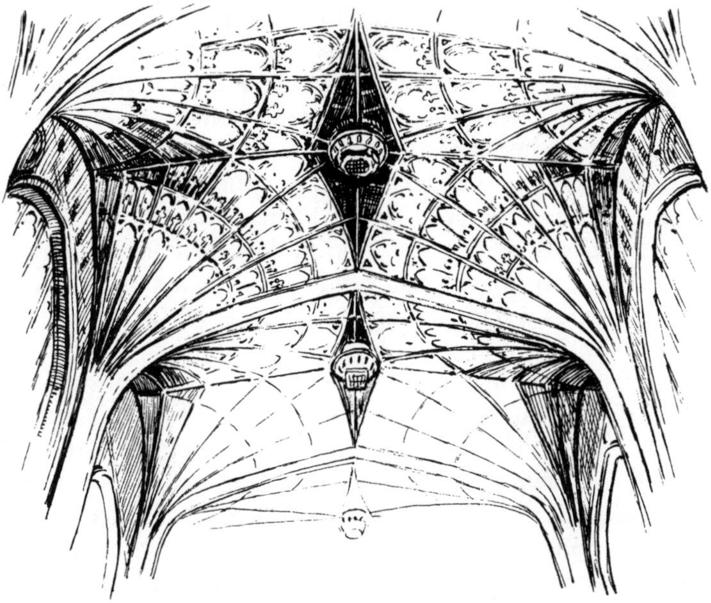

Fig. 3. The fan-vaulted design of this ceiling means that the spandrel—the diamond-shaped centre—*must* exist. It appears central, but does it serve a purpose?

might be the human nose. Man's nose is unlike any other primate's and so one might be tempted to ask 'to what is the human nose adapted? Why is it this shape?' It is conceivable that there is a good, selective, functional explanation for the shape of man's nose, but is it not also possible that the nose is shaped this way simply as an inevitable outcome of an increase in brain size in the ancestral hominid skull? In other words if you expand an ape's brain case and modify the jaw for a particular dentition, you may end up with a human nose (see D'Arcy Thompson's illustration in Chapter 10, p. 156).

By such a metaphor Gould and Lewontin have managed to hint at an explanation for much of organic structure, without having to resort to the selectionist argument that *every* feature, *every* trait has been specifically selected for. Their explanation does not deny the existence of selection or function or adaptation, it simply shifts the emphasis so that features can be seen in context, not individually. This, surely, must be a more realistic approach to nature. Alongside natural selection we can now place other factors also important in determining structure and function: the constraints of history, of development and of architecture. Of course there is such a thing as adaptation—creatures will do all they can to survive—but there are not an infinite number of options open, not a limitless flexibility of design. A creature can only respond with the tools at its disposal, with the genes it has, and so the physical and chemical laws of nature constrain the possibilities.

At any one moment a given creature may be pressured by the environment to respond in a given way. If natural selection were the *only* force acting on the creature then the possibilities open to it would be endless; but we know that the possibilities are strictly limited. They are limited first by what has gone before, by the inheritance of the creature. A given set of genes can only change within certain limits at one go—an insect, for example, cannot suddenly acquire a subtle modification in leaf structure, because it does not have the basic genes for 'leaf' in the first place. The possibilities are limited also by development, by the intricate changes that occur when a set of genes builds a creature. Any change that interferes too violently with the complex and vital changes of early development in the embryo will be lethal or at least damaging. Finally the possibilities are limited by architecture, by engineering and design constraints. A snail shell is spiral and can change in certain aspects of size and shape, but there is a definite architectural constraint on, say, the maximum size a spiral made of calcium carbonate (shell material) can attain. Beyond this limit the organism simply cannot exist without changing other aspects, such as the material used for construction.

> Organisms must be analysed as integrated wholes . . . so constrained by phyletic heritage, pathways of development, and general architecture that the constraints themselves become more interesting and more important in delineating pathways of change than the selective force that may mediate change when it occurs.
>
> *Gould and Lewontin, 1979*

How strong is natural selection?

What Gould and Lewontin are hinting at is really very exciting. Of course, they say, natural selection exists and will determine the sort of direction that adaptation takes. But that is only the beginning—the obvious and least interesting aspect of evolution. The interesting thing is what constrains the changes, what limits the possibilities and determines the final result of selection acting on a creature.

Seen in this light evolution acquires a different meaning. Imagine a creature evolving through time as analogous with a stream running down a mountainside. What is interesting about the stream? Certainly not that it flows: this is an inevitable result of the action of gravity on fluids. What may be of more interest is the path that it takes, or the rate of flow, or the splitting of the stream by a boulder. These are determined by 'constraints' such as the countryside, the steepness of the hill, the soil underlying the stream and so on. In other words the fact of flow (the fact of selection) is uninteresting and is merely an inevitability given the starting conditions (variation in a limited environment). It is time biology moved on to ask more exciting questions about the constraints on evolution, rather than about its driving force.

At this stage it is possible to clear up another misunderstanding about selection. Many biologists ever since Darwin have claimed that natural selection cannot be 'creative' because all it does is limit the existing variation; it does not create anything. This is of course true, but the theory of natural selection actually states that selection *acting on random variations, or mutations,* will effect change. In this sense it can be creative. Take, for example, a car. If one were to alter at random each tiny component on a car and then test the car's performance, one would undoubtedly find that a few alterations actually improved the car's performance (while the majority detracted from it). In that sense selection can act to 'create' a better car, because it is preserving the best features of the machine.

Finally there is one more sense in which natural selection has recently been under scrutiny, although it has not been an argument about *whether* selection can effect change but rather about the way in which selection may effect change.

The Descent of Darwin

One of the biggest problems for Darwin was the explanation of altruism under natural selection. After all, if selection acts to enable the fittest to survive then altruism, or self-sacrifice, is a thoroughly stupid tactic, by definition. When referring to the social insects, which display such obvious altruistic behaviour, Darwin was openly worried. He referred to such behaviour as:

> . . . one special difficulty, which at first appeared to me insuperable, and actually fatal to the whole theory.
>
> *Darwin, 1859*

In the social insects there are several ways in which altruism is manifested: ant, or bee, workers are sterile females which can never reproduce themselves, and yet 'look after' the reproductive females. One often sees mass 'suicides' of social insects, committed apparently for 'the good of the colony'. How can these be explained in terms of the survival of the fittest?

Darwin postulated that in some cases selection could act for the good of the family instead of the individual so that a co-operative family of, say, bees would survive better than an uncooperative family, thus giving rise to social, altruistic behaviour. In this sense natural selection would not act on individuals but on closely related groups. Entire groups would be fitter or less fit, rather than individuals.

This idea was later expanded by Wynne-Edwards, the great British behaviourist and zoologist of the 1950s and 1960s. Wynne-Edwards suggested that selection could even act on large, mixed (i.e. not necessarily closely related), groups or populations to produce co-operative behaviour. Thus a flock of birds, or a herd of wildebeest, which could develop communal safety signals against common enemies, or could develop reproduction strategies to minimize wastage of precious environmental resources, would survive better than a less well co-ordinated group, and in the long run such communal altruistic behaviour would develop.

Although this more expanded version of selection is no longer considered theoretically sound, some palaeontologists have actually suggested very recently that selection can act on entire species. According to this idea of 'species selection' a generalized, highly adaptable, species is more likely to survive for longer than a specialized, less flexible species. Thus the relatively specialized higher mammals such as antelope seem to appear and then become extinct much faster than, say, a species of bacteria. 'Species selection' sounds reasonable, but once more the theoretical basis is not sound and the ideas need refining.

It is only within the last twenty years that the altruism and co-operation of the social insects has been reconciled with the 'survival of the fittest'. It turns out that rather than being an exception to the rule of individual struggle, the ants and bees may just have the whole idea down to a fine art. Because of the breeding system of most social insects the genetic relationship within a colony is very close. Workers, for example, are genetically identical, which means that when a member of the colony 'sacrifices' herself to the 'common good', she is in fact attempting to preserve her own genes. The apparent sacrifice turns out to be an attempt at survival. In the case of such altruistic creatures it is almost as if the individual was irrelevant, as if the genes were the important part. This interpretation has recently assumed great popularity, to the extent that some biologists—most notably Richard Dawkins—have suggested that the 'unit' of selection is not the group, or the family, or even the individual, but rather *the gene*.

Richard Dawkins's *The Selfish Gene* is really an update on Samuel Butler's old adage from the turn of the century that 'the hen is merely the egg's way of ensuring another egg'. According to Dawkins genes use bodies as temporary residences in the long-term battle for survival, and any action selected (on the part of an individual, family, or group) will be one which enhances the gene's chances of survival. This idea is little more than verbal sleight of hand—a clever restatement of the fact that closely related creatures will help one another—and it is misleading in two ways. First it implies that selection can act on single genes in isolation. This seems a ludicrous over-simplification in view of what is understood about gene interaction and the 'cogency' of the genetic compliment of a creature. Second it overlooks the fact that in the majority of creatures selection acts on the entire creature, not on single component parts. How can a single organism acting as a 'prison' for tens of thousands of 'selfish' genes satisfy all their urges at once? And, if all their urges coincide, then why talk of selfish genes at all, why not stick to whole organisms?

*   *   *

The simplistic predictions of neo-Darwinism have not been fulfilled by the growing body of observations of natural selection. Natural selection is extremely difficult to pin down and measure, and what measurements there are suggest that it is less powerful—or at least much less predictable—than was previously expected. Neutralism, the idea that a high proportion of gene variation may have little influence on survival, appears to be a tenable alternative in many, if not most, cases of observed variation. It could be that the whole approach to the study of adaptation has so far been at fault and that the neo-Darwinian obsession with demonstrating selection has been misguided. A study of the factors limiting evolution, such as inheritance, or developmental pathways, or simple architectural or engineering considerations, may prove more fruitful than a continued search for the 'driving force'. It may even turn out that selection is simply uninteresting; not right, or wrong, but merely unilluminating.

Chapter 5

How do new species originate?

———————————— ❈ ————————————

It is an irony of evolutionary genetics that it has made no direct contribution to what Darwin obviously saw as the fundamental problem: the origin of species.

Richard Lewontin, 1974

It is ironic that for all Darwin's scholarship, and despite the title of his major work, the one aspect of evolution he virtually ignored was the 'origin of species', the processes that occur when a new type of creature arises. The principle of natural selection may explain how a population's reserves of variation enable creatures to respond to the environment, and a look at the fossil record may suggest a pattern of major changes over time; but what is it exactly that causes one creature to turn into another? Is natural selection alone sufficient to create a new species, and if so what are the genetic changes which take place? The answers to these, the most basic questions of all evolutionary theory, still remain largely unknown.

The problems surrounding the origin of species are really geographic and genetic. Do species arise by the gradual change of one creature into another or does a parent population have offshoots, as a branch has twigs coming off at the sides? Can a new species arise while it is still interbreeding with the parent population, or is reproductive isolation necessary to avoid 'dilution' of the new genes? If isolation is necessary then how is it accomplished? Is it by geographic isolation in 'islands'? Considering that these questions are still unanswered, it is not surprising that Darwin was unable to tackle the central problem raised by his theory.

The Descent of Darwin

Today, even with the remarkable advances in our understanding of heredity and the structure of the hereditary material, DNA, our knowledge of the genetic events that underlie the origin of species is still sketchy and inconclusive. If anything the problem is now even more perplexing than it was for Darwin, and the most recent advances suggest strongly that natural selection is relegated to a back seat in terms of its shaping power in the origin of species. There is now a shift in emphasis towards abrupt and large-scale change as opposed to the traditional view of evolution as a gradual 'slow-but-sure' process. There is also a new appreciation of the role played by chance, or randomness, as distinct from the very deterministic and functional approach of Darwinists in the past.

The origin of species is called speciation. But what is a species? If you look at the plants and animals inhabiting your back garden, life seems to be organized into discrete, identifiable packets that are fairly easily distinguished: cat, grass, tree, flower, wasp and so on. Even very similar, closely related creatures are usually distinguishable at a glance. A species is a group of plants or animals capable of inter-breeding to produce fertile, viable offspring. In most cases the members of a species are easily recognizable because they look alike, and of course there is a circularity in this: the members of a species look alike because they have vast amounts of genetic material in common; they share this genetic material because they look alike—in other words because they are reproductively and physically compatible. So species are, by and large, self-contained units separated from other life forms by physical and genetic barriers.

When Darwin first suggested his theory of evolution by natural selection he envisaged that the bulk of modification occurred within a lineage, by the gradual transformation of one creature into another as the environment around it changed. Life, to Darwin, was like putty changing shape gradually through time as the forces acting on it altered. He hoped that a thorough study of the fossil record would reveal gradual modification from form to new form over time. The notion was expressed well by the zoologist Seebohm:

How do new species originate?

There is no reason why evolution should not go on indefinitely modifying a species from generation to generation until a preglacial monkey becomes a man.

Seebohm, 1888

Perhaps it was because of this gradualist, within-a-lineage, view of evolution that the idea of speciation did not bother Darwin unduly. He envisaged entire populations changing imperceptibly over vast spans of time to yield new species; and by this view the events taking place at any one moment would be largely irrelevant and immeasurably small. Speciation was, to Darwin, a long-term process involving the slow accumulation of adaptive differences, a gradual moulding of the putty into new shapes and sizes.

Even in the late nineteenth century, however, there were difficulties with this idea. If evolution depends upon the appearance of new variants or mutations to cope with a changing environment, why don't the effects of these variants get 'swamped' by the existing type? For Darwin, as for most British naturalists at that time, inheritance was seen as a blending of parental traits in the offspring. This posed a real difficulty in explaining the spread of a new advantageous variant, or mutant, since at each generation the beneficial effect would be more and more diluted. Although later solved by the Mendelians, this problem led Darwin and his contemporaries to suggest that evolution was accomplished by a gradual shift in the traits of entire populations rather than by discrete individual differences. So rather than single *individuals* being the source of new traits (as Darwin had originally thought), *populations* became the important thing. If the population as a whole could run faster, or keep warmer, or resist disease better than another population, then it would survive.

A second difficulty with this view of evolution within a lineage was the disappointing lack of evidence from the fossil record. Instead of a steady, stately unfolding of creature into creature, for example

species X ⟶ species Y ⟶ species Z ⟶

there was a disjointed and inconclusive record rarely showing

61

the essential intermediate forms between major types. Where were the intermediates? Why did new forms appear abruptly, and disappear without trace?

With a greater understanding of fossils and of the geographic distribution of creatures, it was realized that much of evolution must have been 'branching' as well as 'within-a-lineage'. In this way an increase in diversity through time could be achieved as more and more niches were exploited by new forms of life. Darwin's own interpretation of the Galapagos fauna and flora was based on an increase in diversity due to the spread of species from island to island, from niche to niche. Gradual modification of one form in one place over time might create a new species out of an old one, but it would not increase the overall diversity of life—that could only be achieved by branching of the tree of life.

It was Darwin's disciples more than Darwin himself who fully explored the ideas of adaptive radiation and dispersal, explaining the unfolding complexity of life through the colonization and exploitation of new habitats. And with this study there came a subtle change in the ideas of speciation. Darwin's great disciple Wallace saw evolution as a history of global colonization in which new species arose and spread out to exploit the niches around them through advances and retreats in the face of competition and new, harsh environments. (It is perhaps more than a coincidence that this interpretation arose during the period of Britain's greatest power as a colonial empire.) This assumption is still held today by most biologists.

Ideas of colonization and emigration led to an appreciation of *isolation* as a prerequisite for the origin of species. It was soon realized that a small colonizing population, of even two or three individuals, would enable a rapid adaptation to the new environment without the difficulty of the adaptation being swamped by a huge parent population. New mutations (which might help survival in the habitat) would have a much better chance of being expressed in a small population than in a large one, and of course that would mean that the new colonizing creatures could change rapidly into a new form. In

How do new species originate?

fact it was this realization—that isolation was potentially so important in speciation—that first suggested the relative *unimportance* of natural selection in the origin of species:

> In the principle of isolation we have a principle so fundamental and so universal, that even the great principle of natural selection lies less deep and pervades a region of smaller extent. Equalled only in its importance by the two basal principles of heredity and variation, this principle of isolation constitutes the third pillar of a tripod on which is reared the whole superstructure of organic evolution.
>
> *George Romanes, 1897*

The traditional emphasis on the importance of isolation in the origin of species survives virtually intact to this day. It is the backbone of one of the major theories of speciation still widely held, and one of the central tenets of the modern synthesis of the 1930s and 1940s. Ernst Mayr forged this part of the synthesis at that time, and his belief in the importance of geographic isolation is still highly influential:

> That geographic speciation is the almost exclusive mode of speciation among animals, and most likely the prevailing mode even in plants, is now quite generally accepted.
>
> *Mayr, 1963*

A classic example of such geographic isolation leading to speciation is to be found in the *Larus* gull species of the Northern Hemisphere. In Britain two of the commonest gulls, the lesser black-back and the herring gull, coexist as two separate species. But 'officially' they are the same species since they represent two opposite extremes of a single inter-breeding population. The British lesser black-back *(Larus fuscus)* has a dark upper wing and yellow legs and nests inland on moors. It interbreeds with the Scandinavian lesser black-back. This in turn varies gradually into the Siberian Vega gull of northern Russia and Siberia. The Siberian Vega gull grades into the American herring gull which in turn again cross-breeds with the British herring gull *(Larus argentatus)*. But this gull is distinct from the lesser black-back—it has much lighter wing colour and pink legs—and breeds differently (it is cliff-nesting rather than moor-nesting). So at either end of the 'ring' there are populations which appear to be well on their way to reproductive isolation and ultimately speciation, although they are actually connected by a continuous breeding population around the Arctic. Darwin himself could hardly have asked for a better example of evolution in action. To the 'geographic isolationists' it forcibly demonstrates the principle that environmental forces will vary over a species' range so that peripheral populations will differ and eventually—given isolation, and time, and natural selection—give rise to new species.

This is the basic picture of speciation of the neo-Darwinists, and with a few minor exceptions (such as polyploidy; see p. 70), it is thought to be the underlying cause of all new species. Basically, a parent population splits at its edges into small isolated pockets of a few individuals. Because these pockets are at the edges of the range of the species, the environment is likely to be less hospitable to the creatures and so there is an element of 'colonization in the face of hardship'. As these individuals only possess a tiny fraction of the parental gene pool their potential for change is limited, and at the same time the swamping effect normally facing new variants is reduced. This gives all the ingredients for rapid evolution: small populations, new environments, and strong selection. The fact that the populations are small also means that inbreeding will result, and this will either lead to a rapid demise or it may act to bring out much hidden variability in the creatures. In other words the environment can act rather like a strong artificial breeder—to bring out latent depths of variation which may sometimes be lethal, but which at other times may enable survival in alien surroundings. Also, the new unexploited niche allows a swift population 'flush' because there may be plenty of resources and limited competition. Eventually this leads to new populations quite different from the ancestral ones and, given enough time, the accumulation of sufficient genetic differences to cause reproductive isolation should the new and the old populations meet.

Geographic isolation has been important in the many studied cases where speciation is thought to have occurred, but it is not the only means or prerequisite of speciation, and—as we shall see—there is certainly no justification for the inevitable dogmatism that so often accompanies a good idea:

> . . . divergence to the species-level cannot take place without some prior discontinuity which isolates two sections of the group from each other.
>
> *Julian Huxley, 1953*

Such over-simplification has repeatedly obstructed the progress of evolutionary theory.

Whatever geographic events are necessary to bring about speciation, if indeed they are necessary at all, the basic problem is still one of reproductive isolation, of genetic incompatibility. Species can only be created by the reproductive isolation of two previously interbreeding groups, and in many cases reproductive isolation may be a question, not of geography, but of genetics. Just as the discovery of the Mendelian laws of heredity provided one essential ingredient in the modern synthesis of evolutionary theory, so the most recent advances in genetics and heredity have provided a fresh understanding of how speciation may occur—and this in turn is beginning to undermine many of the old assumptions of neo-Darwinism. It is now clear, for example, that a geographically continuous population of animals may actually consist of 'isolated' groups—isolated not by river or mountain, but by pre- and post-mating barriers due to incompatibility of behaviour and genetics. In fact many of the apparently new and revolutionary upsets to evolutionary theory in the 1980s can be traced back to earlier thinkers whose original ideas met with disagreement and even ridicule in their own day.

At the end of the nineteenth century, when most British biologists were preoccupied with notions of evolution occurring very gradually in large populations, the Dutch botanist Hugo de Vries led the Continental 'mutationists' with ideas of large-scale, abrupt evolution. Whereas the British were trying to show that subtle changes in the characteristics of populations as a whole were the important driving force of evolution, de Vries was convinced that individuals were more important, and that single large mutations could be the origin of new creatures. De Vries studied the evening primrose *Oenothera* and noticed that although there was a recognizable 'normal' type there were also occasional mutants which were physically dissimilar from the parent plants and were automatically reproductively isolated—these mutants 'bred true' and could not interbreed with the parent plants. This abrupt appearance of a new form led de Vries to suggest that evolution proceeded in sudden steps when individuals underwent large mutations.

> The theory of mutation assumes that new species and varieties are produced from existing forms by certain leaps. The parent type itself remains unchanged throughout this process and may repeatedly give birth to new forms.
>
> *de Vries, 1906*

To the British gradualists such ideas were considered ridiculous. Most of the important characteristics that are observed in populations—such as height, or tolerance to temperature, or ability to run—showed continuous variation, not abrupt variation. No single mutation was likely to influence these traits significantly; they appeared to be controlled by many genes in a complex interactive way. Evolution, to them, was a gradual shift in the mean characteristics of a population rather than the sudden appearance of mutants. The debate between the biometricians (who believed in such continuous, subtle change) and the mutationists dominated evolutionary theory at the turn of the century.

What saved the day and enabled both sides to reconcile their differences honourably was the rediscovery, in 1900, of Gregor Mendel's laws of heredity. Mendel had originally shown in the 1860s that variants in the pea plant could be inherited discretely; his work also implied that characteristics were inherited equally from both parents—that they were due to pairs of determinants, one from each parent. After forty years of obscurity (although there are tantalizing rumours that a copy of Mendel's original paper sat in

66

Darwin's study for twenty years) Mendel's work was rediscovered in 1900 and its significance became apparent to both sides in the debate about the origins of species.

The Mendelian theory was a sort of 'half-way house' between the two rival ideas. Variation resided in discrete units—later termed genes—which were individually often of very small effect, and which were inherited directly from both parents. For a given trait—such as eye colour in man—only one of each pair of genes is expressed in the children, the one expressed being called dominant, the other recessive. This forged the way for a unification of ideas since it provided an explanation to satisfy both the mutationists and the biometricians. In the case of the primrose *Oenothera* de Vries had presumably found a single dominant gene of considerable effect that was passed on to offspring. But genes are usually much less dramatic in their effect and for important bodily functions many genes might contribute to an overall effect. So Darwin's idea of natural selection could be seen as acting on discrete units of inheritance that occasionally mutated and were passed on to offspring via Mendel's laws of inheritance. This synthesis is still the corner-stone of neo-Darwinism, and with one or two minor exceptions—like de Vries' primroses—it has allowed the interpretation that speciation is generally due to the accumulation of small genetic differences which eventually lead to reproductive isolation. The most important effect that Mendel's ideas had on the biometricians was that they dispelled the notion that new mutations would be swamped, or diluted, in a population. If variation resided in discrete units, then individuals—rather than entire populations— *could* be the source of new adaptations as de Vries had suggested.

In the neo-Darwinian theory the origin of a new species requires the accumulation—in an offshoot population—of genetic differences, the build-up of new variant genes, so that eventually the offshoot creatures become reproductively isolated from the parent population. The easiest way to encourage the accumulation of gene differences is to separate physically the two populations—hence the popularity of the idea of geographic isolation, and colonization by peripheral groups. A physical barrier between two populations will allow each one to go its own way genetically, perhaps in response to different environmental influences. This is the sort of process that Darwin envisaged with the finches of the Galapagos Islands: small, geographically isolated 'founder' birds would quickly evolve into different forms due to isolation plus selection (see figs. 4 and 5).

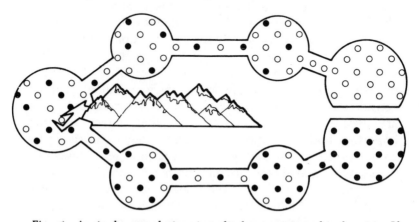

Fig. 4. A single population is split by a geographic barrier. If separated for long enough the two subpopulations may eventually differ enough to prevent interbreeding, even if they mingle.

There are, of course, ways of achieving isolation other than crude physical or geographic barriers. Sexual isolation could lead to a single population becoming two, coexisting in the same habitat at the same time. For instance a simple gene mutation could delay the onset of flowering in a plant and that delay might effectively isolate that plant from the others. In the case of many insects a single gene alteration to a crucial attractant pheromone could mean a loss of attraction to the opposite sex—and once more the insect would be effectively isolated from the others. Of course, such isolation is only the shaky beginning to speciation; in order to survive and reproduce, a sexually reproducing flower or insect requires other creatures with compatible mutations. But in principle

How do new species originate?

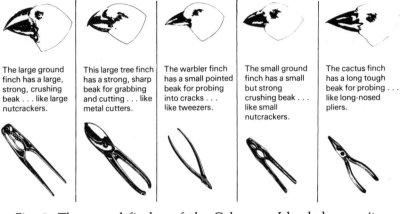

Fig. 5. The several finches of the Galapagos Islands have quite different beak structures. Their beaks are adapted to eating different kinds of food.

quite simple genetic differences could lead to separation and even speciation. This also is part of the classic neo-Darwinian picture of how species originate:

1. Small genetic differences.

2. Isolation (either geographic or sexual).

3. Natural selection (acting in different ways on the two populations).

4. Eventually—given enough time and the accumulation of gene differences—

5. New species.

It is perhaps understandable that the modern synthesis biologists of the 1940s and 1950s felt they had finally conquered the problem of speciation. In fact that impression is quite false. It is rapidly becoming apparent that there are no such simple rules governing the process of speciation. On the contrary, there appear to be many ways by which speciation occurs—some involving isolation, some not; some requiring selection, many not.

Within the last twenty years it has become clear that quite abrupt changes in the structure of chromosomes—changes which appear to have nothing to do with selection *or* geographic isolation—may be a major cause of speciation. Chromosomes are the long strands found in the nucleus of cells which carry the genetic material, the DNA and the genes. The structure of these strands is essential in reproduction and heredity because chromosomes are groups of genes arranged in a specific order.

As it turns out, the sudden appearance of a new primrose species that de Vries noticed almost a century ago was due to a dramatic change in chromosome structure. What had happened was that the entire set of chromosomes within the nucleus had duplicated suddenly, so doubling the total amount of DNA and effectively preventing interbreeding with normal, unduplicated, primroses. This multiplication of chromosome sets is called polyploidy and is clearly a fairly drastic event. In fact one would expect polyploidy to cause more harm than good and, in the case of most animals, it does. But polyploidy may be a major cause of speciation in plants. In the grasses and ferns, for example, over half of all known species are polyploids (whereas among the animals it has only been found in a few fishes, amphibians, worms and molluscs).

The important thing about polyploidy as a cause of speciation is that it requires neither geographic isolation nor natural selection in order to occur. Chromosome duplications appear to be random, unpredictable events (rather like mutations) which are drastic enough to cause isolation sexually but not violent enough (at least in many plants) to cause death. Furthermore it is not only the extreme event of polyploidy which is capable of producing new species; much less dramatic alterations in chromosome structure may underlie many cases of speciation.

Michael White, the Australian biologist who has written the current 'bible' on speciation, recently came to the conclusion that 'very few, if any, closely related species are chromosomally identical'. If you look closely at the chromosomes (as opposed to the genes) of even very similar creatures the chances are that the strands differ in some way—there may be the inversion of a section, or a 'loop' in the strand. These chromosome differences may, according to White, be somehow responsible for the origin of the species in the first place. And that, in turn, means that the origin of species may be an abrupt and random event in which one, or two, or three mutant individuals—mutant in the sense of having the same genes but not the same chromosomal arrangement—become isolated from the parent population by their different chromosome structure. Natural selection certainly plays no part in that scenario, except possibly afterwards when the new species must struggle to survive on its own.

This apparent renaissance in the idea of sudden, drastic speciation is not only prompted by an appreciation of chromosomal change and polyploidy. In at least two related fields recent work has also suggested the importance of chance (as opposed to selection) and suddenness (as opposed to gradualness).

Perhaps the strongest advocate of sudden speciation today is Stephen Jay Gould, a Harvard palaeontologist, who has decided that the abrupt appearances and disappearances of fossils may not be due to gaps in the record, as the neo-Darwinists tend to assume, but rather the actual sudden appearance of new creatures by drastic evolutionary change. Because it is known that polyploidy is rare among animals it must be ruled out as a major cause of large-scale speciation. Gould instead turned his attention to the analysis of development pathways and the timing of crucial stages in growth, such as the onset of sexual maturity, as a possible explanation.

Gould points to living species and asks whether we can envisage gradual intermediate stages giving rise to all the adaptations and features we observe. Frequently, he says, we cannot and must look elsewhere to explain the appearance of such features. An example is found on the island of Mauritius where there are two species of boid snake (a family which includes the pythons and boa constrictors) which share a unique feature: the maxillary bone of the upper jaw is split into front and rear halves connected by a moveable hinge. How, asks Gould, could such a feature have evolved gradually? How can you have *half* a hinge? Such a feature either exists or it does not; there is certainly no apparent intermediate stage, let alone an intermediate with a useful function, for half a hinge. In other words not only is it hard to imagine half a hinge, it is even harder to imagine the functions of half a hinge—what selective pressure would favour such a feature? Gould favours the notion that in such cases a discontinuous transition may have occurred.

This touches a very sensitive nerve of the neo-Darwinists—the whole question of the intermediates between two clearly different functional structures. How does a fin become a hand? How does an arm become a wing? The structural similarity is obvious but the transitional stages are not; it is very difficult to envisage an intermediate arm/wing which would also serve a useful function and be thoroughly integrated with the rest of the creature's anatomy and habits of life. Darwin himself claimed that this was a 'problem of the imagination rather than one of intellect', implying that if we knew more about the fossils and the *possible* intermediates, the difficulty of envisaging transitional forms would disappear. Certainly some convincing intermediates have come to light which help to explain a few of the awkward transitions. The famous *Archaeopteryx* is a fairly convincing intermediate between reptiles and birds with its reptile-like skull and its bird-like wings (see fig. 6). But even here the difficulty of imagining a convincing intermediate between *Archaeopteryx* itself and a full reptile without wings is still formidable. Many biologists would call *Archaeopteryx* a fully fledged bird rather than a true intermediate.

According to the neo-Darwinists such transitions require countless generations and many intermediate species; according to Stephen Jay Gould they may arise considerably faster than that. Gould's attempts to explain rapid change have led him to revive the work of the American geneticist Goldschmidt in the 1930s and 1940s. Goldschmidt, rather in the tradition of de Vries and the mutationists, was unconvinced by neo-Darwinian gradualism and invoked 'hopeful monsters' as the explanation for dramatically new adaptations. Such macromutants would not be caused

Fig. 6. A fully fledged bird or a true intermediate? An artist's reconstruction of *Archaeopteryx*, which was the size of a crow.

necessarily by single mutations of large *direct* effect, but rather by single mutations of great *indirect* effect—genes which were crucial in some regulatory process, which could 'switch' pathways of development or growth and hence cause considerable effect from a minor 'input'.

> This basis is furnished by the existence of mutants producing monstrosities of the required type and the knowledge of embryonic determination, which permits a small rate-change in early embryonic processes to produce a large effect embodying considerable parts of the organism.
>
> *Goldschmidt, 1940*

It is known, for example, that closely related species have very similar genetic constitutions. Man and chimpanzee have over 99 per cent of their genes in common. So why the relatively large differences in, say, the brain or the hands?

Goldschmidt believed that such differences could be due entirely to changes in regulatory genes, which determine rates of bodily growth processes. A computer may be made from thousands of transistors interacting as a complex network, but imagine a single transistor attached to the computer's power supply: any minute change in this regulatory transistor could step up or shut down the entire computer. Similarly a regulatory gene mutation might influence entire bodily systems if they were arranged in such a hierarchical manner. According to such analysis, minor changes in the right place might rearrange an entire creature.

> If it were possible to take judiciously chosen structural genes and put them together in the right relationship with regulatory elements it should be possible to make *any* primate, with some small variations, out of human genes . . .
>
> *Zuckerkandl, 1978*

Changes in such switch or regulatory genes provide a realistic basis for the dramatic reorganization of structure. The American biologist George Oster recently gave an imaginative example of a developmental switch effect to help envisage the evolution of skin structures such as hair, feathers, scales, and teeth. Teeth and hair require the invagination—or folding inwards—of the skin, whereas feathers and scales require evagination—the outward folding—of skin. This suggests that there is not a possible gradual change from, say, a tooth into a scale; the change could *only* occur abruptly:

> . . . this indicates that there cannot be a smooth evolutionary transition between, say, feathers and hair because they are on two separate arms of a binary decision.
>
> *Oster, 1980*

The implication is that a relatively minor gene change could lead to a major switch in development and the appearance of a new feature.

According to Gould small changes in the timing of sexual maturity alone may be sufficient to initiate major morphological changes. He uses the higher primates as examples of this. The head of an adult orang-utan bears little

How do new species originate?

physical similarity to the head of an adult human, but the head of a juvenile orang-utan is strikingly similar to that of an adult human. The likeness is strong, and suggests a fascinating explanation of man's evolution (see fig. 7, and also Chapter 9, p. 149-50). Could it be that man has evolved from his ape-like ancestors not by the selection of particular traits such as hairlessness or large brain, but simply by the earlier onset of sexual maturity? Since other aspects of growth tend to stop when sexual maturity is reached, it is possible to alter a creature by delaying or speeding up sexual maturity. Might this explain why an adult man looks so like a juvenile orang-utan? Gould has suggested that human evolution has entailed neoteny—that is the increasingly early onset of sexual maturity—leading to adult humans resembling ancestral juveniles. Could such an event lead to the origin of new species?

> If we do not invoke discontinuous change by small alterations in rates of development, I do not see how most major evolutionary transitions can be accomplished at all.
>
> *Gould, 1978*

Fig. 7. A baby and an adult chimpanzee. The young chimp—like the young orang-utan—bears a striking similarity to man.

The drastic means of speciation so far dealt with—polyploidy, chromosomal rearrangement and Gould's changes in developmental timing—are of as yet unproven importance in animal evolution. Many animal geneticists staunchly rely on the traditional geographic isolation model as still the most economical, claiming that polyploidy is almost exclusively a plant phenomenon, that chromosomal rearrangement may well be a result of speciation rather than a cause, and that changes in timing, or regulation, are undocumented except for a few amphibians, such as the axolotl. This rather narrow view of speciation is unlikely to persist, however, in the face of the latest developments in genetics.

Ever since the discovery of vast amounts of repetitive, or so-called 'junk', DNA in plants and animals, geneticists have sought an explanation for its existence. Why should nature, normally so conservative and economical, fill up the crucial genetic 'blueprint' of creatures with vast amounts of apparently useless repetitive sequences of DNA? Some have suggested that these repeats are simply genetic junk—useless leftovers of normal genetic processes. Others have thought that the repeats may be 'selfish', that they serve no useful function but 'hitch-hike' on the normal DNA parasitically. Still others have suggested that these repeats are there to allow experimentation by the genome, to allow new variant genes to be attempted without interfering with the normal working of the genes. The most recent explanation, and the most exciting, suggests that the repeats are actually responsible for creating new species.

Gabriel Dover and his colleagues at Cambridge University have studied the repeats and found that they are divided into 'families' so that a particular sequence may be repeated hundreds or thousands of times in any one set of chromosomes. What is intriguing is that these families of identical repeats are constantly being 'homogenized' within a creature *and* within a species so that all the members of a family *remain* identical. Obviously this homogenization can only occur within breeding populations, and the result is that members of any one species are instantly recognizable by their repeat families. Even closely related species of, say, *Drosophila* fruit fly, which may be largely identical in their structural, unrepeated, genes, are instantly recognizable as different in their repeated sequences. Since these repeat families make up a large proportion of the genome, the fact that they are constantly being homogenized may act to help interbreeding within a population (since genetic compatibility would be high). Dover has suggested that it is the repeat families which ensure the 'wholeness' of the species—allow interbreeding within a species—and prevent cross-breeding with other creatures that have different 'families'. The repeats make up so much of the genome—well over 95 per cent is not an uncommon proportion—that any minor differences in these repeats could cause irrevocable reproductive breakdown. Now, imagine two parts of one huge population, at opposite ends of the range. If the homogenization at one end were to differ very slightly from the homogenization at the other, one could imagine these slightly different families spreading out and finally meeting in the middle of the range like ripples in a pond. And, because the families differed, the two parts of the same species might be genetically incompatible: a new species is in the making. Hence the origin of species might be due to random differences in the repeat sequences, and not have anything to do with the actual structural genes which are the building blocks of the animal. This mode of evolution has been termed 'horizontal' or 'concerted' evolution by Dover and his colleagues because of the rapid spread or homogenization of sequences which appears to defy Mendelian laws of segregation.

> This would be the beginning of the inception of reproductive isolation: an accidental consequence of the spread of different sequence patterns between the chromosomes of two separate groups of sexually reproducing individuals. We are proposing that reproductive isolation is not necessarily a consequence of adaptation to separate environments . . .
>
> *Dover et al., 1980*

Once again the onset of species-formation may be abrupt and need not be related to natural selection directly, and again we can see how the importance of natural selection has gradually diminished as a fuller understanding of speciation has been reached. Darwin originally saw selection as the prime mover of evolution, gradually changing one creature into another over time. That is no longer thought to happen. To begin with, geographic and reproductive isolation are considered important (even essential by the neo-Darwinists), which diminishes the role of selection. More recently the ideas of polyploidy, chromosomal changes and switches in development have all reinforced the element of sudden chance in speciation. Dover's ideas of homogenization can be seen as yet another denial of the importance of gradual selection since it too is, in Dover's own words, 'not necessarily a consequence of adaptation'.

The overall message of speciation is one of many causes and no simple solutions. There are convincing examples of gradual speciation and abrupt speciation, of speciation requiring geographic isolation and speciation requiring none; of gene mutations leading to reproductive isolation and of chromosomal alterations leading to reproductive isolation.

Finally, the assumption that natural selection is the prime mover of speciation no longer underlies our understanding of evolution. Natural selection may explain the origin of adaptations, but it cannot explain the origin of species.

Chapter 6

Why don't we see gradual transition in the fossils?

———————— ❄ ————————

The geological record is extremely imperfect and this fact will to a large extent explain why we do not find interminable varieties, connecting together all the extinct and existing forms of life by the finest graduated steps. He who rejects these views on the nature of the geological record, will rightly reject my whole theory. ·

Charles Darwin, 1859

Certainly the record is poor, but the jerkiness you see is not the result of gaps, it is the consequence of the jerky mode of evolutionary change.

Stephen Jay Gould, 1980

For Charles Darwin the single most important source of evidence in support of natural selection lay in the fossil record. He considered it crucial that a thorough study· of fossil remains should reveal a pattern consistent with his ideas of gradual transformation. It is therefore highly significant that a large proportion—perhaps even a majority—of leading palaeontologists today disagree with Darwin's interpretation of the tempo of evolution. The essence of the disagreement is that the fossil record does not reveal a slow, steady unfolding of life through time but rather a sporadic picture of sudden appearances and mass extinctions, of gradual transformation alongside abrupt discontinuities. Darwin believed the difficulty lay in the imperfection of the fossil record; modern palaeontologists feel the difficulty lies largely in neo-Darwinism.

Long before Darwin popularized the notion of evolution

geologists realized that fossils existed and represented the remains of once-living creatures. So long as these creatures bore a close similarity to living ones there was no difficulty interpreting them: death does not run counter to any 'natural theology' and, at a pinch, it was possible to argue that all such past remains had lived and perished within the 6,000 years estimated to have elapsed since Genesis (in the seventeenth century Bishop Ussher had even calculated that the Creation had occurred in early October, 4004 B.C.). Problems began to arise when it was realized that the fossil record represented a history of past events stretching back much further than a few thousand years, and that many of the fossil creatures bore no resemblance whatever to living ones. Why should God have gone to the trouble to create a species only to allow it to die out? This *did* run counter to theology. In the first half of the nineteenth century there were basically two opposing schools of thought that attempted to explain the fossil record: the 'catastrophists' and the 'uniformitarians'. To a surprising extent the present conflict can be seen as a direct descendant of the disagreement between these two schools 150 years ago.

Georges Cuvier, the influential French anatomist and geologist, was the leading catastrophist. During the early nineteenth century, in the years following—and deeply influenced by—the French Revolution, Cuvier proposed the idea that the geological history of the world was punctuated by great revolutions or catastrophes which had caused the extinction of vast numbers of species. Rather than invoke successive creations to explain the restocking of life following these episodes, he imagined radiations and migrations from unaffected regions. In other words he envisaged a single act of creation followed by a series of catastrophes which had caused partial extinctions. For Cuvier this explained the appearance of the geologic strata accurately: long periods of relative stability interspersed with abrupt changes.

In strong opposition to these views, the Englishman Charles Lyell became the leader of the uniformitarians with the publication of his *Principles of Geology* between 1830 and 1833. Lyell believed that it was unreasonable to invoke massive, unknown forces in explaining the past; rather one should attempt to reconstruct history in terms of known present-day influences. So such gradual forces as wind, tide, and water-flow in rivers were considered a sufficient explanation for the geologic past. The abrupt discontinuities of geology were admitted by the uniformitarians, but were seen as long periods of non-deposition of sediments, rather than as catastrophes. For Lyell an abrupt change in geology did not necessarily reflect some environmental cataclysm, rather it could be the result of a gradual change in climate, or flow of a river, or the drying up of a lake bed. Perhaps Lyell's greatest contribution was his appreciation of the great age of the earth. This allowed for the possibility that all the dramatic changes in the earth's history could have resulted from the accumulation of gradual effects acting over vast expanses of time, rather than the abrupt changes invoked by Cuvier. Lyell did admit the appearance and disappearance of species but saw these as successive creations and extinctions, or as migrations, rather than as a 'progressive' change; he believed that all the *main* forms of life had existed from the beginning (see fig. 8, p. 87).

Darwin was strongly influenced in his early thinking by Lyell. When he set sail on the *Beagle* in 1831 Darwin had a copy of the newly published *Principles of Geology* with him and there are frequent references to it throughout his notebooks from the voyage. It is certainly not only in his geological thinking that Darwin was influenced by Lyell; in the second volume of the *Principles* Lyell discussed at length the theory of organic evolution proposed by Lamarck, and the importance of geology to any such theory. Of course Lyell did not believe in evolution (even thirty years later he was to disagree vehemently with Darwin's proposal for the origin of species), but he instilled in the young Darwin an almost religious belief in the power of gradualism in geology.

Lyell's uniformitarianism came to dominate British geology in the mid-nineteenth century whereas Cuvier's catastrophism held sway on the Continent, especially in France. It is hardly surprising, therefore, that the idea of gradualism should underpin *The Origin of Species*. Evolution

6a

is a historic process, and history as revealed by the geologic strata was seen as steady and gradual. The evolution of life, therefore, was gradual. This belief became one of the implicit assumptions of Darwinism, and neo-Darwinism. In 1942 Julian Huxley, one of the architects of the modern synthesis of neo-Darwinism, reaffirmed this faith unquestioningly:

> In all cases where fossils are abundantly preserved over a considerable period, we find the same phenomena. The change of form is very gradual.
>
> *Huxley, 1942*

> The palaeontologist is confronted with forms which gradually and continuously change their characters in the course of time, until they become so different that they merit a new name.
>
> *Huxley, 1951*

Such comments are typical of the traditional Darwinist approach to the question of the fossil record, and until a few years ago this gradualism remained unchallenged by the majority of evolutionists.

To show the extent of the present dispute over the tempo of evolution, here are two quotations from Stephen Jay Gould, an equally typical representative of the new generation of palaeontologists who disagree with Lyellian gradualism:

> For millions of years species remain unchanged in the fossil record, and they then abruptly disappear, to be replaced by something that is substantially different but clearly related.
>
> *Gould, 1980*

> . . . gradualism is a culturally conditioned prejudice, not a fact of nature.
>
> *Gould, 1978*

How could two leading evolutionists hold such diametrically opposed opinions? What *is* the message of the fossil record— gradualism or abrupt change?

If it were possible simply to dig into the earth's surface and retrace the history of an area chronologically with increasing depth, there would be no problem. Presumably one would find a fossilized history of life for that area showing the evolution of forms all the way from the simplest of creatures.

What one actually finds is nothing like this. The fossil record is patchy and discontinuous, and in no one area is there more than a tiny fraction of geologic time recorded for us to interpret. The world's geologic record is like a ruler that has been chopped into thousands of short sections and then scattered around randomly—it is sometimes very difficult to work out the exact sequence of the original. In the case of the fossil record, however, the difficulty is even greater than for our chopped-up ruler, for several reasons.

First, a fossil record only exists for sporadic parts of time and space because fossils represent dead plants and animals which are embedded in a sedimentary deposit such as a river bed or a coastal estuary. Whenever and wherever erosive (rather than sedimentary) forces have acted there will be no fossils to find. Similarly only certain rocks contain fossils; rocks that have originated from volcanic sources, or that have been exposed to immense temperatures or pressures, will not contain fossils. So at best the fossils we find are only the remains of those creatures that were 'in the right place at the right time'. This explains why the record is so scattered and incomplete, since the right conditions are unlikely to exist in the same place for very long.

Second, the fossil record can only represent a fraction of all living creatures in any one place or time because fossilization only occurs when there is hard bony or woody tissue. A fossil becomes a fossil because hard parts decay more slowly than the sediments building up around them so that a mould, or cast, is created which is filled up by further deposits seeping in. Any creature that is composed solely of soft parts—that is the great majority of all plants, and a significant proportion of all animals—will never be preserved. This severely limits any interpretation of the evolution of early life, because the proportion of species having hard parts is thought to have increased with time.

Third, the interpretation of the fossil record is very difficult because both the earth's surface and most creatures on it are mobile. One cannot assume that the fossil one finds on, say, the West African coast today was actually once a West

African coastal creature. Continental drift has moved the earth's land masses around like blocks of ice on a pond. It is now known, for example, that for hundreds of millions of years (until 80-100 million years ago) West Africa was joined to South America roughly along the present coastal borders, so that fossils dating from that era are likely to be found in both areas. This fact is obviously crucial to any interpretation of African/South American evolutionary lineages; until continental drift was appreciated the existence of similar creatures in West Africa and South America was assumed to be evidence of transoceanic migration or dispersal. This is no longer necessary. Conversely, when one finds the abrupt appearance, or disappearance, of a fossil form in geologic strata it is important not to ignore the possibility of migration from one region to another. Present-day birds and mammals are known to move around seasonally in search of food or territory, and sudden migrations (such as the recent spread of locusts through the eastern Sahara) commonly occur, so presumably such events have happened in the past. The sudden appearance of a new creature in the fossil record does not therefore automatically imply sudden evolution (or creation).

We can add to these three major difficulties of interpreting the fossil record the further thoughts that:

1. Even in the periods of sedimentation the correct chemical balance is required for fossilization.

2. Once a fossil has been formed it must remain intact (i.e. uneroded and undestroyed) until a palaeontologist finds it.

3. The fossil beds now known represent only a tiny fraction of all there are.

4. Even under optimum conditions only certain features, or parts, of fossilized plants and animals have been preserved for modern-day study.

So we can see that the fossil record of evolution is at best a tangled web that is open to interpretation. That abrupt changes in geology and fossils exist is clear; that these changes reflect actual catastrophes or, on the other hand, are

The fossil record

mere artifacts of an imperfect record is still open to opinion.

As in so many of the present problems of evolutionary theory, Darwin himself was perfectly aware of the difficulties of interpreting the fossil record. Because of his gradualist bias Darwin suggested that the only reason we do *not* see a slow, steady, unfolding of life through time is the imperfection of the fossil record.

> Geology assuredly does not reveal any such finely-graduated organic chain; and this, perhaps, is the most obvious and serious objection which can be urged against the theory. The explanation lies, as I believe, in the extreme imperfection of the geological record.
>
> *Darwin, 1859*

Perhaps the most vivid metaphor of all for the fossil record is due to Darwin himself:

> I look at the geological record as a history of the world imperfectly kept, and written in a changing dialect; of this history we possess the last volume alone, relating only to two or three countries. Of this volume only here and there a short chapter has been preserved; and of each page only here and there a few lines. Each word . . . may represent the forms of life.
>
> *Darwin, 1859*

It is this interpretation—that the only reason we miss all the myriad intermediates in evolutionary history is due to the imperfection of the record—which was inherited by the neo-Darwinists. But it is no longer the prevailing opinion among palaeontologists.

In the early 1970s several leading American palaeontologists started to express the opinion that, despite the obvious imperfections of the fossil record, Darwin's picture was basically wrong and that evolution appeared to proceed not gradually but in fits and starts. The main proponents, Steven Stanley, Niles Eldredge and Stephen Jay Gould, coined the term 'punctuated equilibria' to express the pattern as they saw it—long periods of stasis during which little obvious change is seen in a species, punctuated by abrupt disappearances or replacements by distinct, if related, forms. In other words the absence of intermediates is not due to 'missing pages' in the story but is a fact of evolution implying abrupt large-scale changes in creatures.

It had always been recognized, by even the most ardent of gradualists, that geologic history was at times abrupt in the very large-scale sense. The relatively sudden demise of thousands of marine and terrestrial species—including the dinosaurs—at the end of the Cretaceous period, for example, has always been a puzzle to evolutionists. Yet that is quite different. Mass extinction is difficult to explain by *any* theory, but it in no way denies a general philosophy of gradual transformation; it is merely an admission that occasionally the environment may act quite suddenly to weed out many species at once.

A more serious large-scale problem is the sudden appearance, about 650 million years ago, of representatives of virtually all the known types of animal (in fact the only missing type is backboned creatures). This 'Cambrian explosion' has puzzled palaeontologists for over a century, although the conventional explanations have centred, once more, on the inadequacies of the record before the Cambrian period. But, like the Cretaceous extinctions, this was not seen as any threat to Darwin's principles of transformation.

The theory of punctuated equilibria, on the other hand, has been seen as a direct assault on neo-Darwinism because it suggests that, far from being exceptions to the gradual rule, these abrupt extinctions and appearances are typical of the entire fossil record (see fig. 8). The idea of stasis—that species tend to remain constant over the main duration of their existence—implies that evolution is not gradual but sporadic, and it questions the power of the environment as the main shaping force of life. Do environments remain constant for millions of years and then change abruptly? The claims for sudden change are also controversial because of the implication that the speed of evolution is too rapid for conventional neo-Darwinism to explain. There has even been talk (as mentioned in Chapter 5) of macromutation and the old notion of 'hopeful monsters' to explain the sudden appearances of new creatures.

The fossil record

B. *Darwin* (gradual change)

C. *Eldredge & Gould* (punctuated equilibria)

Fig. 8. The same fossil pattern may be interpreted in different ways: as separate, unconnected creatures (A), as a 'tree' of ancestry (B), or with connections but also with abrupt appearances (C).

The controversy, however, cannot be seen in terms of black and white. The extent to which both the advocates of this new outlook and the neo-Darwinist defendants consider these ideas as undermining evolutionary theory varies a great deal. At the least extreme end of the spectrum there is the claim for a pluralistic approach to the problem. Evolutionary change may occur both gradually (because, after all, there are some convincing examples of gradual transition in fossil forms suggesting slow, steady evolution) and erratically. Even cases of erratic change, of 'punctuated equilibria', need not necessarily contradict neo-Darwinism. As we saw in Chapter 5, it is generally assumed that small populations of species at the edge of their range may become isolated and undergo fairly rapid genetic divergence from the parent population. Such isolated populations may then succeed in their new environment and even spread back to out-compete the parent population. Such a chain of events would lead to an apparent abrupt evolution in the fossil record although no neo-Darwinian rules have been broken. The intermediate forms do exist, it is just that they are only present in small peripheral populations.

At the other end of the spectrum is the blatantly rebellious interpretation:

> The history of any one part of the earth, like the life of a soldier, consists of long periods of boredom and short periods of terror.
>
> *Gould, 1980*

Palaeontologists such as Gould claim that the abrupt appearances of new species in the fossil record are *real* and not artifacts. Why should we invoke migrations and unknown inadequacies of geology to explain the observations of sudden change? Is it not more scientific to accept the observations at face value and attempt to explain them? It is at this point that talk of hopeful monsters and abrupt genetic change arises, to coincide neatly with the current debate on speciation and the arguments about which mechanisms underlie the origin of species. There are certainly tantalizing parallels between some of the most recent ideas on abrupt speciation and the modern palaeontologists' discontent with the old-fashioned gradualist views of fossil history. And although the palaeontologist's work has no direct dependence upon evolutionary theory *per se*, the dissatisfaction with neo-Darwinism among several palaeontologists is palpable.

> Punctuationists do not deny the operation of natural selection but suspect that it may substantially be confined to adaptational

'fine-tuning' to the environment, and believe that extra-polation to processes of species formation may not be warranted.

Hallam, 1981

Several of them interpret the stasis of the fossil record as being the small-scale tracking of the environment by a population; minor fluctuations in environment causing minor morphological change in a creature. Such minor changes, they are prepared to admit, may be controlled by selection, but this, they say, is quite separate from speciation.

I think I can see what is breaking down in evolutionary theory—the strict construction of the modern synthesis with its belief in pervasive adaptation, gradualism and extrapolation by smooth continuity from causes of change in local populations to major trends and transitions in the history of life.

Gould, 1980

The responses to the claims for punctuated evolution have ranged from paranoia to perplexity with a variety of reactions in between. From extreme traditional quarters have come accusations that the punctuationists are playing into the hands of the creationists due to the obvious implications of 'sudden appearance' and the inadequacy of neo-Darwinism. A more original—but equally extreme—criticism of the approach is that it is (either wittingly or not) a manifestation of Marxism because of its revolutionary underpinnings. Although abrupt discontinuities are typical of a revolutionary process, to suggest that some palaeontologists are deliberately superimposing Marxism on fossils seems far-fetched (although this is not to deny that habits of thought can influence our perception of the world—see Chapter 10).

The strongest scientific response to ideas of erratic evolution has come predictably from the population geneticists. They are at the 'pit-face' of the evolutionary process, observing populations responding slowly to environmental forces, and are hesitant to admit that what they can see at the population level—the gradual trans-formation of populations in the laboratory—may have no relevance to the 'macroevolutionary' level. Their argument is a strong one because of the vast and convincing body of observations of creatures responding to their environment adaptively. Many of them are simply unconvinced by the apparent swiftness or abruptness of change in the fossil record.

> A new species arising in 50,000 years (2 metres of sediment) is sudden to a palaeontologist but gradual to a geneticist.
>
> *Maynard Smith, 1980*

Fifty or one hundred thousand years may be a single bedding plane to a geologist, it may represent only a tiny fraction of a cliff face or a geologic epoch, but it is nevertheless tens of thousands of generations in the lineage of, say, a marine snail, and is therefore more than enough time for gradual neo-Darwinian evolution to act. Certainly the notion of sudden jumps by macromutation is considered out of the question by the population geneticists. Apart from the fact that there is little evidence for macromutations or abrupt switches in development, the very idea is anathema:

> . . . it would be like trying to perform a surgical operation with a mechanically controlled scalpel which could only be moved a foot at a time.
>
> *Maynard Smith, 1981*

Maynard Smith also attacks the palaeontologists for not providing enough raw fossil evidence for their claims. He considers that gradual transformation is as much (if not more frequent) a feature of the fossil record as is punctuated change. To be sure, the hard data brought to bear on either side of the issue has been scanty and inconclusive.

Something that the neo-Darwinists do seem ready to admit is the difficulty of explaining stasis—if indeed stasis turns out to be a general phenomenon. According to traditional views such stability would only be found when competition, predation, food chains, and other features of the environment were also stable. But how likely is this over periods of hundreds of thousands or even millions of years? Most ecologists would say that it is pretty unlikely. Another possible explanation (discussed more fully in Chapter 9) for such stability is that either the genetics or the developmental biology (or both) of creatures will only allow certain paths to be followed morphologically. In other words once a species has found a successful solution to environmental problems it will stick to it through many minor genetic changes and perturbations and will only change when another stable, successful solution has been reached. This implies that there are severe constraints on evolutionary change and that only certain genetic combinations are going to make a viable creature. Once again this contradicts the neo-Darwinian approach which would predict that genes may act singly to the extent that creatures are capable of responding (given enough time) to *any* subtle changes in environment. This notion of genetic and developmental constraint is crucial to evolutionary theory because of the implication that not all conceivable solutions to problems are possible. If this were generally true the importance of natural selection would be diminished to a fine-tuning role rather than as an omnipotent moulding force.

John Maynard Smith has countered this argument by saying that if species were really caught in 'ruts' due to constraints of genetics or development we would not expect to see the large degrees of morphological variation in species that we do, especially in species of wide geographical distribution. Sure enough certain species of wide distribution, such as the *Larus* gulls of the Northern Hemisphere (see Chapter 5, p. 63-4), show gradual physical changes over their range to such an extent that those gulls at the extremities behave as two distinct species despite the fact that all the intervening populations are perfectly interfertile. But the problem is not that easy; species such as the *Larus* gulls may well be exceptional. In the majority of species such gradual variation is not seen and all the members are equally interfertile.

Where does this leave us? It appears that convincing examples of both gradual and punctuated evolution can be furnished from the fossil record, so there is no valid reason to discard a theory proposing gradual change. On the other hand if the punctuated examples are real and not artifacts due to migration or geology itself, then evolutionary theory must address itself to the problem of explaining rapid bursts of evolution. An open-minded pluralism does seem necessary pending further evidence.

It is at this stage entertaining to realize that there is really nothing new in this debate whatsoever. Here is Darwin on the difficulties of finding transitional fossil forms:

> It is a more important consideration . . . that the period during which each species underwent modification, though long as measured by years, was probably short in comparison with that period during which it remained without undergoing any change.
>
> *Darwin, 1859*

Once again Darwin anticipated the present dispute. What is astonishing, however, is that thirty years *before* Darwin the same problem was considered, and intuitively explained, by one of the several anticipators of Darwin's theory of natural selection, Patrick Mathew. In 1831 Mathew, a total outsider to the zoological fraternity, published a treatise on *Naval Timber and Arboriculture* in which the following passage is found:

> [catastrophic events] . . . must have reduced existence so much that an unoccupied field would be formed for new diverging ramifications of life . . . these remnants in the course of time moulding and accommodating their being anew to the change of circumstances, and to every possible means of subsistence—and the millions of ages of regularity which appear to have followed between the epochs, probably after this accommodation was completed, affording fossil deposit or regular specific character.
>
> *Mathew, 1831*

Surprisingly, 'punctuated equilibria' is only one of several claims from the new generation of palaeontologists and in some ways it is not the most controversial, even though it has received the widest press. The 'macroevolutionists' have several other challenging ideas to confront the neo-Darwinists with.

The fossil record

The first is the apparent *scala naturae* that exists for the longevity of species. Just as individuals have life expectancies that are fairly predictable, so it would appear that species too have life expectancies related to their complexity. In short, the simpler the creature, the longer that creature is likely to remain in the fossil record. A simple creature will persist for longer than a more complex, 'highly evolved', one. The duration for a plankton in the fossil record may be about twenty-five million years; that for a mammal may be as short as a few hundreds of thousands of years. But why? Out of such observations there seems to be emerging a theory of 'species selection'—a sort of large-scale natural selection—that predicts which kinds of species are most likely to survive under various environmental conditions. Just as a particular type of individual may survive best in one environment, so a particular type of species may be better adapted to survive the vagaries of geologic time. This is certainly not Darwinian or neo-Darwinian, although it does not necessarily contradict the spirit of Darwin's natural selection.

A much more shocking opinion that appears to be quietly gaining ground among palaeontologists is the idea that progressive evolution—increasing diversity over time—is far from apparent in the fossil record. A recent research textbook, *Patterns of Evolution*, has the following comment in the concluding remarks:

> . . . we reach the new conclusion that many palaeontologists seem to regard total diversity as being close to a steady state.
>
> *Schopf, 1977*

This implies that the tree of life has stopped spreading its branches, that a sort of equilibrium has been reached where the amount of diversity of life is no longer increasing. This idea stems from the observation that for most groups studied there does not appear to have been any increase in species diversity throughout their geologic histories. Combined with the perennially puzzling fact that nine-tenths of all animal phyla are to be found right back in the Cambrian period—among the earliest remains of the 'Cambrian explosion' of 650 million years ago—this opinion is bound to make the evolutionists uneasy. Steady state theory in evolution is rather like the flat-earth theory of pre-Copernican astronomy—it is simply outrageous in the present day. (It is also interesting that in the same concluding chapter of *Patterns of Evolution* it was tallied that twelve of the sixteen contributors favoured a punctuationist as opposed to a gradualist interpretation of fossil change.)

In conclusion, there is a growing feeling among leading palaeontologists that the fossil record shows patterns which are not predicted from our understanding of populations and of small-scale processes. Whether punctuated equilibria is a more accurate description than gradualism is almost irrelevant—it is clear that both patterns are found and that, at a pinch, both patterns can be reconciled with neo-Darwinism. A variable rate for evolution may contradict some of the more dogmatic neo-Darwinists, but it does no injury to Darwinism itself. The large-scale ideas of species selection and species 'life expectancy' are more difficult to explain in terms of neo-Darwinism but once more may only require an adjunct to the theory rather than a change. The apparent preference for a steady state interpretation of evolution is really very provocative and may prove a bitter battleground in the future. I think the fairest comment to end this chapter on is by Richard Lewontin. At a time when most geneticists are polarized against the new palaeontological fashion, Lewontin has observed:

> As an evolutionary geneticist, I do not see how the origin of higher taxa are the necessary consequence of neo-Darwinism.
> *Lewontin, 1980*

The message seems to be that while the theory of natural selection is not actually contradicted by the researches of the macroevolutionists, it may simply prove inadequate in explaining the large-scale events, which, after all, it was originally designed to explain. Perhaps the laws governing the large-scale events—such as the origin of new types or the extinctions of species—are different from those governing the very small-scale processes, so that the population geneticists should not guard so jealously *all* aspects of evolution. The fossil hunters may have their own contribution to make to evolutionary theory.

Chapter 7

Can we separate pattern from process?

————————————— ✳ —————————————

In my view the most important outcome of cladistics is that a simple, even naïve method of discovering the groups of systematics—what used to be called the natural system—has led some of us to realise that much of today's explanation of nature, in terms of neo-Darwinism or the synthetic theory, may be empty rhetoric.

Colin Patterson, 1980

What the creationists have insisted on for years is now being openly advertised by the Natural History Museum.

Beverly Halstead, 1980

'Cladistics' is a word seldom heard outside biological circles —and is poorly understood even within them—yet it represents a set of ideas exerting a profound influence in the small, but in terms of evolution crucial area of systematics. Cladistics (from the Greek word *klados*: branch or shoot) is a way of classifying the living world into groups: animal, vegetable or mineral; bird, reptile or fish. A harmless enough occupation you might think, except that through cladistics some biologists have come to doubt the value of Darwinian ideas. If Darwin added the dimension of time to classification—by proposing a historical process to explain the groups—the cladists are threatening to take it away again. For this reason cladism has become a battle-front for neo-Darwinism.

Long before Darwin suggested a process to explain the pattern of nature, naturalists had tried to identify and classify the incredible diversity of living things. This practice—of which Linnaeus was undoubtedly the most famous exponent—is known as systematics, or taxonomy, and is a shining example of man's obsessive desire to collect, to identify, to catalogue the objects in the world. If one is confronted with a random assortment of creatures including, say, an oak tree, a snail, a frog, a birch tree, and a kangaroo, there are at least a few obvious similarities and differences that enable groupings to be made. The oak and the birch, for example, have a lot more in common with each other (a thick vertical trunk with branches and green leaves) than with a frog; and a frog and a kangaroo have a basically similar design, with four limbs and a central backbone, that the others don't share. So on the simplest and most superficial of observations one might lump the creatures as follows:

1. Oak and birch
2. Frog and kangaroo
3. Snail

Similarly there is a clear 'scale of nature' from the simple (a single-celled amoeba, for example) to the complex (a higher vertebrate with hundreds of millions of co-ordinated, differentiated cells). It is therefore possible to classify plants and animals into groups and hierarchies based only on a study of structure. That is the first important point about *any* means of classification; it is quite possible to classify life solely on the basis of what you see in front of you—you don't need to know how the features arose in the first place.

Any theory of evolutionary descent must suggest a process by which this pattern of nature has arisen, but the pattern really came first in the sense that 'the study of things caused must precede the study of the causes of things'. It is therefore hardly surprising that the system of classification of living creatures that now prevails, after more than a century of Darwinism, bears a striking similarity to the taxonomies which existed before Darwin, even dating back to Aristotle's *Scala Naturae*. Aristotle proposed a linear (rather than a modern, branching) classification based on the principle of 'perfection'—roughly analogous to our modern conception of

97

complexity. And of course man himself was at the top of the scale:

1. Man
2. Viviparous quadrupeds (e.g. horse)
3. Whales
4. Birds
5. Amphibians and reptiles
6. Serpents
7. Fishes
8. Cephalopods (e.g. squid)
9. Crustaceans (e.g. shrimp)
10. Insects and spiders
11. Molluscs (e.g. snail) and echinoderms (e.g. starfish)
12. Sponges
13. Plants
14. Inanimate nature

It is interesting to note that Aristotle actually included man in his taxonomy, admitting that man is an animal, and also the marked similarity between this scale and later classifications which were based on extensive studies of comparative anatomy unknown to Aristotle.

The very fact that Aristotle's scale of nature is so like our own present-day classification shows that evolutionary theory is not essential to the everyday work of the taxonomist. Similarly you do not need to know the history of the motor car to be a good mechanic. But it is this very idea—that you can separate the process of nature from the pattern—which has caused considerable offence to the neo-Darwinists. As we shall see, some of the cladistic taxonomists believe quite strongly that not only can you separate pattern from process, but that you *must* do so if you are to be an objective taxonomist.

The history of systematics since Aristotle shows a trend toward greater objectivity in classification with the advances in understanding of comparative structure and function. It may be straightforward to classify a snail in relation to a tree or a mammal, but determining relationships among a closely knit group (such as tiger, leopard, puma, lion) is much harder and demands a comprehensive knowledge of anatomy and physiology. It is no good trying to classify on the basis of only a few characteristics; this will just lead to discrepancies and later difficulties. When the great Linnaeus came to organizing the plant kingdom, in his *Systema Naturae* of 1735, he decided to use the sexual structures alone as the criterion for groupings. This led to some, by present-day standards, totally artificial groups because he had not taken enough aspects of structure and function into account. The obvious way to classify creatures is to put them together in the same class if they share the same characteristics—for example size, shape, bone structure, and so on. A difficulty arises, however, in deciding which characteristics are important. Take, for example, a gorilla, a man, and a mouse. If you look only at body hair you would put the gorilla and the mouse together in the same class—because they are both brown and hairy—and man into a different one. If you decided this was absurd and that body size is more important, you would put man and gorilla into the same class—which may seem more sensible, but it is still not enough. A consideration of size alone could lead you to classify together, say, a mouse, a sparrow, and certain lizards because they are all small and weigh a few ounces. Yet in other respects they are quite unrelated. So a good classification looks at many characteristics and decides which ones are important and which are not.

Cladistics is a method of doing that. It makes the practice of taxonomy rigorous and exacting because it forces the scientist to be objective and to sort out important from unimportant features of plants and animals. In this way relationships between creatures are discerned by the application of clearly defined rules rather than at the whim of the scientist.

So far, there is nothing controversial. Cladistics is an advance in the science of taxonomy and even the staunchest Darwinists are quick to praise its use. The trouble is that this newly found rigour in taxonomy has led some of the cladists to ask wider questions. The first of these questions is: do we need evolutionary ideas when we classify? The implicit assumption of the Darwinist is most certainly, yes!

The Descent of Darwin

> . . . the tree of life must be erect not pressed on paper, to
> study the corresponding points.
>
> *Darwin, 1859*

Darwin's influence on systematics was profound. With the acceptance of evolution came two important realizations. First that species were changeable rather than fixed, immutable entities and, second, that every creature—whether alive or dead—represents a tiny part of a huge tree of life.

> . . . our classifications will come to be, as far as they can be
> so made, genealogies; and will then truly give what may be
> called the plan of creation.
>
> *Darwin, 1859*

The groups of creatures which had previously been lumped together because of anatomical similarities suddenly became related descendants from common ancestors sharing features *because* of their descent. Fossil forms were suddenly seen as possible dead ancestors rather than as stillborn creations or the victims of past catastrophes. Similarities of structure were now seen as a clue to common ancestry, whereas differences of structure were due to divergence at some stage in the past. The flat, two-dimensional classifications of Aristotle and Linnaeus suddenly sprang to three-dimensional life with the addition of time and descent.

At least at first glance an appreciation of evolution helps one to visualize a tree of life and explain the obvious similarities between many groups in nature. Certainly, in many instances, the existence of a fossil record has enabled lineages and relationships to be worked out. When the fossil of *Archaeopteryx*—a reptile with wings and feathers—was found in the Bavarian limestone in the 1860s, it seemed an obvious intermediate between the ancient reptiles and the more recent birds, and therefore a probable ancestor of the birds. Even Darwin himself was quite delighted with the discovery and understandably so. Surely such fossils, and even living intermediates, enable us to re-create the past history of life?

There are, however, real problems associated with the use

of fossils in classification, and it is the cladists' solution to these problems that has caused some of the present controversy. If we had a complete fossil record of all the creatures that could potentially have been fossilized in the past, we would still be very poorly off in taxonomic terms because a vast proportion of species (most plants, for example) are composed solely of soft parts which are not preserved in stone, and also because even the hard bony parts of, say, a dinosaur tell us little of physiological function, or internal organs, or the creature's behaviour. As it happens the fossil record, far from being complete, is very sparse and sporadic—only a tiny fraction of potentially fossilized creatures are represented (see also Chapter 6, p. 83-5). What is more important, the remains—individual plants or animals—that do exist are hardly ever complete enough to enable a reliable re-creation of structure.

What is the taxonomist to do? To give bone fragments the same importance in classification as sophisticated techniques of comparative embryology, biochemistry or genetics in living organisms seems ludicrous for all but the crudest of purposes, and yet to ignore the fossil record entirely as a guide to relationship because it is incomplete would seem like throwing out the baby with bath-water.

However, it is not only the incompleteness of the fossil record that bothers the cladists; to some cladists the very idea of ancestry itself is unscientific because we simply do not have the ability to know that such-and-such a fossil really is an ancestor.

The idea of ancestry turns out to be a kind of logical trap. It seemed to the early Darwinians, and presumably to many Darwinians now, that building up the tree of life was just a matter of time, a matter of finding the right fossils, linking them up in the correct ways and before long the whole history of life would be there before us as revealed truth or unshake-able fact. It never worked out like that and it wasn't until the development of cladistics that anyone realised why that was. And the reason is a fairly simple one: one recognises relationship between organisms by characters but there is nothing one can say about an ancestor that will relate it to its descendants—the concept of ancestry is not accessible by the tools we have. One can search out one's own ancestry by means of parish registers and so on, but going further back into the past there's no handle to get hold of, no way of doing it.

Patterson, 1981

Ideally classification should express descent exactly, but our only really reliable criteria for classification come from living plants and animals—the descendants. It is therefore impossible to re-create descent accurately. The cladists suggest that perhaps taxonomists should not be constrained by the unattainable ideal of reflecting descent, but should rather concentrate more on sorting out the relationships among *living* creatures. Some cladists go further and claim that evolutionary theories to explain the existing pattern are premature until our understanding of that pattern is much more complete.

. . . we are hardly likely to achieve any understanding of the evolutionary process until we have achieved an understanding of the pattern produced by that process and . . . even today we have hardly begun to understand the pattern.

Platnick, 1980

To cladists such as Platnick and Patterson evolutionary theory is not only unnecessary for good taxonomy, it can actively hinder the understanding of nature with its pre-conceived ideas of relationship built up from pitifully little fossil evidence. Recently, for example, there has been news of a true fossil bird that pre-dates *Archaeopteryx*. In this way a single fossil may destroy an entire story that has been—falsely as it turns out—constructed to explain how one type evolved into another type. A general suspicion of evolutionary 'stories' is now felt by many cladists. Although the principles of classification espoused by the cladists have been widely welcomed and adopted by taxonomists, this divorce of evolution from taxonomy, and the implied doubts about neo-Darwinism, have caused fierce argument among other biologists.

The cladistic school was founded by the German

systematist Willi Hennig in the early 1960s. The principles are simple and sensible: suppose you want to determine the relationships between a lizard, a kangaroo, and a rat. The first principle of cladistics is that 'two groups are more closely related to one another than to a third group when the two groups share a homology not shared with the third'. So we must seek features shared by two of the three creatures. There is no point in looking at characters found on only one of the creatures (say, the kangaroo's pouch) because that will tell you nothing about their relationships. Similarly there is no point in examining features that are the same in all three (say, a vertebral column). You must seek homologies, or shared characters, such as skin structure, reproduction, or aspects of anatomy; in all three the rat and kangaroo can be seen to share characters not found in the lizard and are thus more closely related. The features used in determining these relationships are not fixed but are relative depending on what is being compared. If an insect is to be compared with the lizard/kangaroo/rat then clearly the vertebral column becomes a criterion for grouping whereas before it was not. Similarly the criterion of possessing hair, or mammary glands, becomes useless if comparing, say, kangaroo/rat/rabbit because all three have these features.

Undoubtedly the single most controversial assumption of cladistic taxonomy is that no creature can be classified as an ancestor to any other creature (see fig. 9). A series of closely related creatures are always grouped 'equally'. In other words the three species A, B, C can only be related in one of three ways; a cladist would never assume that one was ancestral to another.

In the study of *living* creatures this assumption is uncontroversial because no existing species can be ancestral to another existing species—although they may be related via a recent common ancestor. (Although the zebra and the horse may be very close in terms of descent, no one would argue that the zebra descended from the *present-day* horse; it may, however, have descended from a recent ancestor of the modern horse.) It is in the application of cladist taxonomy to fossils that the arguments arise. Cladists maintain that even if

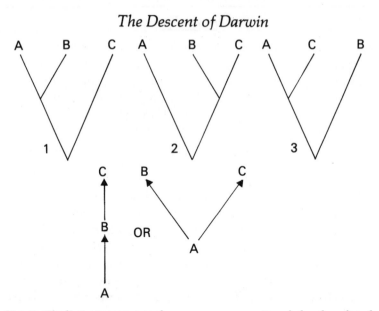

Fig. 9. Cladistic taxonomy always groups a series of closely related creatures 'equally' (1-3 above). A cladist would never assume that one creature was ancestral to another (below).

there is enough information to enable fossil classification, it is unscientific and unreasonable to assume any ancestral links.

A classic example of the perils of classifying fossils can be seen in the descent of man. Each time a new hominid skull, or femur, is unearthed the anthropologists try to reconstruct the hominid lineage to accommodate the new find. But the results can never be certain because, as we have seen over the last ten years, a new discovery is always capable of upsetting the current fashionable interpretation. Within less than a year of the transmission of his 'definitive' television series, *The Making of Mankind*, the anthropologist Richard Leakey was already disagreeing with some of his own earlier theories. Even when the story of how a particular creature evolved looks watertight, we can never be scientifically satisfied that the correct picture has been drawn. Not only is the fossil record pitifully inadequate, but we have no way of knowing that a particular creature actually is an ancestor of another. What has happened is that a basic working assumption of cladistics—that creatures should be classified without assumptions of ancestry—has led to doubts about the very idea of ancestry itself:

> The question is naturally asked: why do cladists refuse to accept ancestors? This question is most often asked by palaeontologists who designate fossils as ancestor and depict them in evolutionary trees. The questions that a cladist would ask in return would be: How do we recognise ancestors? How do we test an hypothesis of ancestry? What do we gain by proposing such hypotheses in the first place?
>
> *Forey, 1981*

This is, of course, the point at which the floodgates open and the tide of cladism meets neo-Darwinism with much frothing and foaming. The evolutionists are prepared to concede that the cladists can classify without evolutionary theory playing any role, but to start denying the existence of ancestors altogether is simply too much. Literally thousands of books have been written by biologists exploring ancestry—the origin of life, the rise and fall of the dinosaurs, the descent of man. To those cladists who reject ancestry such works are little more than fiction, and the Darwinian explanations of how past creatures have come into existence and gone to extinction are largely unfounded.

> As it turns out all one can learn about the history of life is learned from systematics, from the groupings one finds in nature. The rest of it is story-telling of one sort or another. We have access to the tips of the tree; the tree itself is theory, and people who pretend to know about the tree and to describe what went on in it—how the branches came off and the twigs came off—are, I think, telling stories.
>
> *Patterson, 1981*

Clearly some cladists, such as Peter Forey and Colin Patterson from the Natural History Museum in London, are rejecting the role of evolutionary theory in taxonomy, and there are strong hints of a more general rejection of neo-Darwinism altogether. It is therefore hardly surprising that there has raged a 'great cladist debate' in the pages of *Nature*, one of the world's leading scientific journals, over the past three years. The correspondence pages of *Nature* have become the forum for a continuing argument about cladism and the cladists that has at times been vociferous, at times funny, but always entertaining.

At the end of 1980 the palaeontologist and staunch 'old-school' taxonomist Beverly Halstead, in a broadside attack on the cladists at the Natural History Museum, accused one of the newly opened exhibits, the 'Origin of Man' exhibit, of indirectly supporting the creationists with the assumption that no hominid fossil could be said to be ancestral to man. He went further:

> If the cladistic approach becomes established as the received wisdom, then a fundamentally Marxist view of the history of life will have been incorporated into a key element of the educational system of this country.
>
> *Halstead, 1980*

Halstead's remarkable use of the word 'Marxist' here appears to arise from a misunderstanding on his part; he may have confounded cladism with the other current revival in ideas of the abrupt appearance and disappearance of fossils (see Chapter 6) which certainly do betray a revolutionary, 'Marxist' approach to evolution. But Halstead was not alone in his attack. Another aspect of the Natural History Museum's 'Origin of Man' exhibit which caused a stir was the use of the expression 'If the theory of evolution is true . . .'.

In response to this John Maddox, *Nature*'s polemical editor, wrote a scathing editorial:

> If the words are to be taken seriously, the rot at the Museum has gone further than Halstead ever thought.
>
> *Maddox, 1981*

He also warned the Museum to 'beware of selling out on Darwinism'. At this stage the debate, hitherto restricted to the cladist enclave at the Natural History Museum and their supposedly 'subversive' influence on the public exhibits, opened into a more far-ranging argument about the value of neo-Darwinism as a scientific theory.

What are we to make of the cladist debate? Are the extreme

cladists—those who reject notions of ancestry and view neo-Darwinism with suspicion—harbingers of a new post-Darwinian biology, or are they as hopelessly out of touch as Halstead and Maddox maintain?

We can see how they have come to doubt neo-Darwinism. Cladistics is an advance in taxonomy because of its rigour, and that rigour has caused some soul-searching over fossils and ancestry. This soul-searching in turn led to a closer look at the neo-Darwinian theory itself and, so it would seem, the worst suspicions were confirmed: the theory was not capable of explaining the past. At this point the cladists look to other aspects of evolutionary theory which are being challenged—the doubts about speciation, the uncertainty about rates of evolutionary change—and draw the conclusion that they are indeed justified in their own doubts, since so many other aspects of neo-Darwinism are also now in question. But have these extreme cladists gone too far?

Cladistic taxonomy has become widely accepted because it provides an objective and powerful means of discerning relationships among creatures. One of the beneficial results has been a 'spring clean' of traditional ideas so that glib and groundless assumptions about ancestry and adaptation are now frowned upon. But there are cladists who stop at this point. To them the extreme cladists, who now reject neo-Darwinism *in toto*, have overstepped the mark. It is one thing to say 'be careful when you propose ancestry', but quite another to say 'ancestors can *never* be found'. It is admirable to be a purist and say 'let's study pattern before we propose a process', but it is simply naïve to divorce theory from observation so completely. The neo-Darwinian process, for all its flaws and abuses, remains the only viable framework within which to view life. If the cladists have an alternative process then let them propose it, but surely it would be mistaken to reject the entirety of natural selection without providing an alternative. To such a comment I suspect the extreme cladists would reply: 'Neo-Darwinism does not explain the origin of species in the first place; it is only by clearing our minds of it that we can hope to observe nature's pattern objectively.'

The Descent of Darwin

In a sense it is time alone that will judge the cladists. If selection theory does fade in importance they may be viewed in twenty years as the harbingers of a new objectivity; if neo-Darwinism recovers from the attacks the cladists will undoubtedly be seen as a 'nutty clique' who 'didn't really understand natural selection anyway'.

Whether the cladist revolt against neo-Darwinism endures or not, the stance must be seen in context. Not only does the cladist attack coincide with a period of doubt about other—both scientific and philosophical—aspects of neo-Darwinism, but it can be seen as the revival of a tradition in biology. In 1917 the great biologist D'Arcy Thompson wrote:

> The physicist explains in terms of the properties of matter, and classifies according to a mathematical analysis . . . and his task ends there. But when such forms, such conformations and configurations, occur among *living* things, then at once the biologist introduces his concepts of heredity, of historical evolution, of succession in time . . . of common origin of similar forms remotely separated by geographic space or geologic time, of fitness for a function, of adaptation to an environment, of higher and lower, for 'better' and 'worse'. This is the fundamental difference between the 'explanations' of the physicists and those of the biologist.
>
> *D'Arcy Thompson, 1917*

In his way D'Arcy Thompson would have hailed the cladists. Like them, he was concerned more with the study of form than with premature explanations of how the form 'evolved'. Physicists drew up a periodic table of the elements long before any explanation was attempted to account for it; we still have no convincing explanation for the evolution of the elements, but we do have the periodic table.

The neo-Darwinists look on the extreme cladists as hopeless cases, biologists who have lost their way. But to a large extent I think they have been misunderstood. If you probe beneath the surface sensationalism of 'rejecting ancestry', of 'playing into the hands of the creationists', men such as Patterson are not actually saying that the neo-Darwinian explanations are necessarily wrong, rather that the theory may turn out to be largely irrelevant to the progress of biology:

> Just as pre-Darwinian biology was carried out by people whose faith was in the Creator and His plan, post-Darwinian biology is being carried out by people whose faith is in, almost, the deity of Darwin. They've seen their task as to elaborate his theory and to fill in the gaps in it, to fill in the trunk and twigs of the tree. But it seems to me that the theoretical framework has very little impact on the actual progress of the work in biological research. In a way some aspects of Darwinism and of neo-Darwinism seem to me to have held back the progress of science . . . There is an extraordinary ferment going on within evolutionary biology at the moment. Where it will lead I wouldn't pretend to guess. I think that the general theory—that evolution has taken place—will remain, but that more people may come to realise that it is not essential to doing biological research to believe in it.
>
> *Patterson, 1981*

If the cladists' doubts were the only cloud in the evolutionary skies we could ignore them more easily.

Chapter 8

Can genes learn from experience?

———————— �֍ ————————

In effect, only two theories of evolution have ever been put
forward: one, originating with Lamarck . . . the other,
originating with Darwin . . .

John Maynard Smith, 1966

When individuals of any species change their situation,
climate, mode of being or habits, their structure, form,
organisation, and in fact their whole being becomes little by
little modified till in the course of time it responds to the
change experienced by the creature . . . so that after many
successive generations, these individuals, which were
originally, we will say, of any given species, become
transformed into another one.

Jean Baptiste de Lamarck, 1809

One of the attacks on the existing evolutionary dogma that
has attracted the most attention is the recent revival of
Lamarckism. In fact Lamarckian revivals were fashionable
before Charles Darwin even put pen to paper. The recent
renaissance is only the latest in a long series. One can hardly
be surprised, reading the quotation above, that Lamarck's
ideas of transformation have persisted so tenaciously. To all
but the experienced biologist those lines could easily have
been written by Darwin himself. They certainly share some
fundamental ideas: environmental pressure, gradual
transformation, adaptation, even the origin of new species.
Yet in terms of mechanism the similarity is superficial:
Lamarck proposed—in the same year that Darwin was
born—a mechanism of evolution unrelated to Darwin's
subsequent notions of natural selection. Lamarck's idea was

Can genes learn?

that adaptive modifications acquired by a creature during its life could be passed on directly to its offspring.

In 1979 the great philosopher of science Karl Popper was invited to choose the book that he considered the most interesting published that year. His unexpected choice was a thin volume by a then unknown Australian immunologist called Edward Steele, entitled *Somatic Selection and Adaptive Evolution: On the inheritance of acquired characters.* In it Steele outlined a radical departure from neo-Darwinism by suggesting that Lamarckian inheritance may occur as a matter of course in the immune systems of animals, and conceivably may underly *all* inheritance to some extent. Steele proposed, and later claimed to have successfully performed, experiments demonstrating the inheritance of acquired characters—the central tenet of Lamarckism—in laboratory animals. He even went so far as to dismiss existing neo-Darwinist theory as '. . . a rather crude conceptual device and unlikely to be the final word on the evolution of multi-cellular organisms . . .'. It was a grand gesture somehow typical of the Lamarckian tradition; a tradition involving shadowy names such as Kammerer and Lysenko—scientists whose attempts to vindicate Lamarck ended in ignominy. So far, Steele's work has met with an eerily similar fate.

Jean Baptiste Pierre Antoine de Monet, Chevalier de Lamarck, like so many naturalists of the eighteenth and nineteenth centuries, seems almost to have stumbled upon biology after disappointments in the more orthodox gentlemanly pursuits of theology, medicine, or the military. The first exceptional thing about Lamarck was that he tried all three before being inspired, reputedly by the romantic philosopher Jean Jacques Rousseau, to study nature. Lamarck went on to become one of France's leading biologists, and was appointed Professor of Invertebrate Zoology at Paris's prestigious Musée d'Histoire Naturelle in 1794. But it was not until 1809, with the publication of his *Philosophie Zoologique*, that Lamarck, then a man of 65, proposed a theory of evolution.

Perhaps the best introduction to Lamarck's contribution to

the study of life is a passage from Charles Darwin in *The Origin of Species:*

> He first did the eminent service of arousing attention to the probability of all change in the organic, as well as the inorganic, world being the result of law and not of miraculous interposition.
>
> *Darwin, 1872*

It is ironic that this very role, of substituting biology for theology, is so often ascribed to Darwin himself. Considering that Lamarck was thinking about, and even proposing mechanisms for, organic change fifty years before Darwin, Lamarck's contribution has been consistently underrated. Or perhaps it would be more accurate to say that Darwin's contribution may have been overrated.

It is a common misconception to attribute not only the theory of natural selection to Darwin, but also the theory of evolution. In fact one could argue quite convincingly that neither, strictly speaking, originated with Darwin, although he was the first to put them together as cause and effect. Evolution, the idea that life has undergone a succession of forms through descent, can be seen clearly in the writings of several late eighteenth-century thinkers such as Buffon, Hutton, and even Charles' own grandfather, Erasmus Darwin:

> Shall we then say that the vegetable living filament was originally different from that of each tribe of animals . . .? Or as the earth and ocean were probably peopled with vegetable productions long before the existence of animals; and many families of these animals, long before other families of them, shall we conjecture that one and the same kind of living filament is and has been the cause of all organic life?
>
> *Darwin, 1794*

Since the living filament' that Erasmus Darwin refers to was meant to imply 'formative' (or 'heriditary') material, it is clear that he was suggesting some sort of organic evolution. Such ideas were becoming common currency (although were not necessarily accepted) at the end of the eighteenth and start of the nineteenth century.

Can genes learn?

Lamarck was the first to suggest the means by which life may have evolved. In the *Philosophie Zoologique* he suggested that the production of new anatomical or physiological features results from a 'need' (*besoin*) felt by the creature in response to the environment, and that everything acquired or changed during an individual's lifetime is preserved by heredity and transmitted to that individual's offspring. This is the essence of Lamarckism: the inheritance of acquired characters.

Suppose you are a blacksmith, constantly using your arms. Is it not natural, argued Lamarck, that your muscles will grow in response to that need? Is it not also possible that this increased muscle potential might be transmitted to your children? Might this not explain the gradual transformation, over countless generations, of creatures as they come to terms with environmental change? The traditional example of Lamarckian evolution is the long neck of the giraffe. Faced with food shortage on the arid African savannah, the ancestral giraffe responded by stretching its neck upwards, eventually leading to the evolution of the present-day creature. The need gave rise to a heritable response and ultimately to a new species.

Lamarck's contribution to biology extends beyond this idea of the inheritance of acquired characters. He was a brilliant invertebrate biologist and taxonomist; much of his classification remains to this day. He was also probably the first biologist to point out that living systems tend towards increasing complexity with time. But, inevitably, it was his novel mechanism of evolution that created his reputation. It also brought him ridicule—then as, so often, now. In the early nineteenth century the most influential French naturalist—apart from Lamarck himself—was the brilliant anatomist Georges Cuvier. Through his exhaustive studies of the comparative structure of both fossil and living vertebrates, Cuvier had developed his own theories about the past history of the earth which conflicted sharply with Lamarck's views (see Chapter 6, p. 80). Cuvier was aware of the changes in fauna to be found in the fossil record and explained them in terms of successive catastrophes (of which

113

Noah's flood was the most recent) causing mass extinctions. He did not invoke new species (whether 'evolved' or 'created') to replace extinct forms but suggested migrations and radiations to account for the succession. Lamarck's notion of gradual transformation was openly scorned by Cuvier; after all, if life has evolved gradually why are there such gaps in the fossil record and where are the intermediate forms? Cuvier denied the existence of such intermediates—an opinion still found among palaeontologists and one that still causes argument. Because of his greater academic power, Cuvier's catastrophism prevailed in the early nineteenth century and Lamarck, like his ideas, sank into obscurity. It was only with the general realization, by the mid-nineteenth century, that evolution *had* occurred, that Lamarck rose again.

The appeal of Lamarckism is clear, and extends beyond the apparently objective realms of science. If a creature is capable not only of a positive response to its environment, but also of transmitting this response to its offspring, then evolutionary change is a *directed* process. A creature can positively adapt to its surroundings without having to wait passively for a rare, random mutation that just happens to benefit it at the time (but is much more likely to harm it). According to neo-Darwinism, or more accurately, Mendelian genetics, beneficial or adaptive change in the genes can only result from random events, so that the individual is imprisoned by the limitations of his genes. Underneath the science there also lies a philosophical statement. It is hardly surprising that Lamarck's ideas, because they are so fundamental to any interpretation of life, should arouse strong feelings. So it has been: the history of Lamarck's theory over the past century and a half has been a convoluted tale involving character assassinations, frauds—real or imagined—and even suicides. At least in Britain and the United States any Lamarckian leanings have been treated as eccentric and ill-informed, a manifestation of hopeless romanticism. Edward Steele certainly met these attitudes with his recent attempt to revive Lamarck.

Lamarck's original theory involved two stages: first, the

114

acquisition of a new character through 'need' and, second, the transmission of that character to offspring. Steele claimed to have evidence for both. Although several independent attempts to repeat Steele's results have now failed, it is revealing to trace his fortunes and the response of the scientific community to his controversial ideas.

It has been known for over twenty years that animals are capable of learning a new immunological 'trick' if they are taught it early enough in life. Normally any attempt to graft, or transplant, tissues from one creature to another—even if closely related—fails because of rejection by the host body. The immune system of the host identifies the transplanted tissue as foreign, just as it might identify a flu virus or infective bacterium, and a rejection response takes place to rid the body of the invading material. In fact specific molecules—called antibodies—are synthesized by the animal to counteract the invading substances—called antigens. It is through this bodily defence system that animals can protect themselves from disease.

The new trick, discovered in the 1950s, was that laboratory mice can actually acquire the ability to tolerate foreign transplanted tissue if exposed to it from an early age. Suppose you start out with two unrelated groups of mice, A and B; if you attempt to transplant tissue from adult B to unrelated adult A, rejection will result. But if you transplant from adult B to an unrelated *young* mouse A, then that mouse acquires the ability to tolerate the transplant so that when it becomes adult no adverse reaction to B tissues occurs (see fig. 10).

A simple analogy would be to present two middle-aged men with a complex problem in calculus. If one of the men had no prior knowledge of mathematics he would undoubtedly reject the problem as insoluble. If the other man had received a good mathematical training at school, the chances are that he might struggle towards an answer. He would have 'acquired tolerance' to calculus. The two men may have had equal potential for calculus, but it had not been equally exploited, and hence the unequal result.

The discovery of acquired immunological tolerance brought the Nobel Prize for Medicine in 1960 to Sir Peter

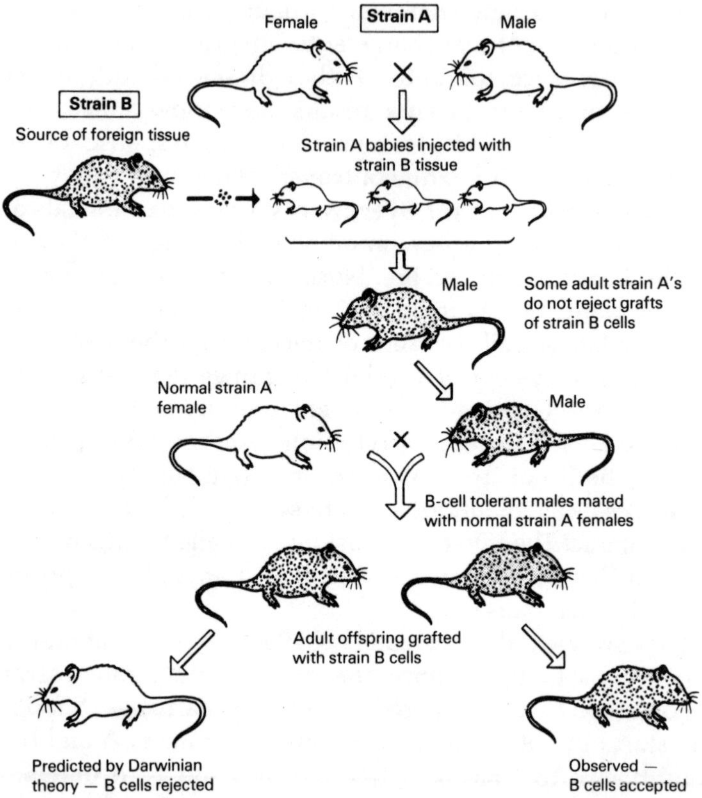

Fig. 10. The experiment by Steele and Gorczynski on the inheritance of acquired characters. Has tolerance to foreign cells been passed on to offspring? (After Hitching)

Medawar and his co-workers. So it is apt that, on hearing of Steele's ideas, it was Medawar who offered Steele the opportunity to confirm and continue his research in England. Steele accepted.

Steele claimed vigorously to have gone one vital step further than Medawar and his colleagues with their acquired tolerance. In a pair of research reports written with Reg Gorczynski in 1980 and 1981, Steele published data showing clearly that acquired tolerance had been transmitted to offspring. Cells from one group of mice had been injected into newly born mice of an unrelated group; as expected, these mice acquired tolerance to the first group's cells. The tolerant mice were raised to adulthood and then their offspring were studied. The remarkable finding was that the offspring showed similar tolerance to the other group's cells *without themselves having been exposed to such cells.* The acquired tolerance had been transmitted to offspring—or so Steele and Gorczynski claimed.

To return to our analogy of the two men struggling over the calculus problem: it was as if the man who could solve the problem because of his early training had passed this ability on to his children, who would have it automatically, without the need for lessons in mathematics. What parent wouldn't wish for such a mechanism of inheritance!

Medawar, and soon the whole immunological fraternity, was excited. This was Lamarckism. This contradicted the established laws of Mendelian inheritance taught to all biologists at an early age. Was Steele right? If so, was Mendel wrong? Throughout 1980 and 1981, while Steele and several independent workers tried to repeat the original experiments, the biological world buzzed with a variety of reactions to the claims for a Lamarckian revival. Several of the more established immunologists openly expressed doubts about Steele's claims, but everyone awaited the results of the repeat experiments with interest.

From the start Steele's claims for Lamarckian inheritance were bound to run into deep trouble from the orthodox neo-Darwinists. It is simply not possible, for example, to suggest that Mendelian inheritance is wrong. Modern genetics works, and has worked for seventy years, successfully on the basis that Mendel was essentially right. According to Mendelian genetics, a creature's characteristics—such as immunological tolerance—are determined by the complement of genes it possesses, and this complement is fixed at fertilization by the fusion of sperm and egg. There is no question of changing genes half-way through life; the moment you are conceived not only is your own genetic make-up determined, but also your contribution to your future offspring. You are blue-eyed because both your parents are blue-eyed; you cannot start out with one set of genes and end life with a different set, let alone transmit a new set of genes to your children. If this happened then most of the experiments breeding cows, or wheat, or roses, just would not work the way they do. At best, the Mendelians would say, Lamarckism is the exception rather than the rule.

In 1981 and 1982 several papers were published in the journals, notably *Nature*, casting severe doubts on Steele's work. The repeat experiments failed to find transmission of the acquired tolerance to offspring, and Steele's original data were questioned openly. There was even a suggestion that Steele had, perhaps unwittingly, selected data to favour his expectations. Another major criticism was that even if his results had been repeated, the conditions of the original experiments (involving, for example, injecting tens of millions of cells into new-born mice, which is about one-tenth of their body weight) were so extreme as to render any conclusions irrelevant to conditions in the real world. There was a sudden crystallization of attitudes. The immunological world seemed perceptibly to close ranks on the shady outsider and his sporadic followers. After a brief period of unemployment in the summer of 1981, Steele returned to Australia protesting strongly that the new evidence did *not* contradict his original claim. Yet, as several repeat attempts have since failed to show any inheritance of acquired tolerance, there are few supporters of this Lamarckian revival left.

There is a weird irony about the whole Steele episode, and a strong sense of *déjà vu*. In 1926 the Austrian biologist Paul Kammerer committed suicide after accusations of fraud were levelled at his experiments purporting to demonstrate Lamarckian inheritance in the footpads of the midwife toad.

Kammerer, without doubt a respected and accomplished experimental biologist, had devoted his career to the study of inheritance and claimed to have found convincing examples of Lamarckism in several species. The results which Kammerer himself considered most convincing involved not the midwife toad (which rejoices in the delightful name of *Alytes obstetricans*) but the primitive sea squirt *Ciona*

118

intestinalis. Ciona lives on the ocean floor and possesses two tubular siphons which wave around above it, one for the intake of sea water, the other for its expulsion. Kammerer cut the siphons and found that the creature replaced them with longer ones, and claimed that the offspring inherited these longer tubes. The work was not accepted by the scientific community, although faithful repeats of his experiments were not carried out—and have not been carried out since. We will probably never know whether Kammerer actually perpetrated the discovered fraud that led to his suicide, but it seems a pity to have allowed potentially interesting research to die with the man.

In the 1930s and 1940s the reputation of the eminent psychologist William McDougall suffered a blow when he claimed to have evidence that rats can inherit the acquired ability to tackle mazes; subsequent experiments threw doubt upon the result. McDougall had exposed rats to a maze problem and counted the number of attempts required to learn the solution. He then did the same with the offspring of these animals, and with their offspring in turn and so on, and found a decrease in the number of attempts required to master the maze. The experiment lasted fifteen years, spanning over thirty generations of rats, and the results are striking. In the first generation the rats averaged over 200 errors before mastering the problem; this had dropped to about 80 in the tenth generation, and to under 40 in the twentieth generation (see fig. 11). In fact McDougall himself was decidedly cautious in his interpretation of the results; he suggested Lamarckian transmission but admitted that other effects may have contributed, such as unconscious selection of proficient rats. His colleagues were less cautious. Several attempts were made by other psychologists to repeat the work and some succeeded, yet the Lamarckian interpretation was rejected. No other explanation was found and there is still none (but see Rupert Sheldrake's hypothesis in Chapter 9, p. 141-3).

More recently, in the 1940s and 1950s, the infamous Lysenko led Russian biology up a scientific blind alley with his hope that Lamarckian inheritance would enable wheat to

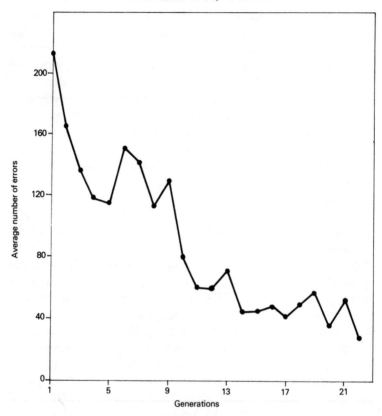

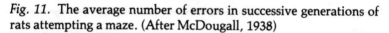

Fig. 11. The average number of errors in successive generations of rats attempting a maze. (After McDougall, 1938)

prosper on the barren steppes. In Lysenko's case, however, the motive for promoting Lamarck was clearly political rather than scientific. Darwin and Mendel had come to represent 'capitalist' science, and Lamarck was seen as more 'Marxist' in approach, presumably because Lamarckism represented greater hope of achieving a directed change (just as Marx had hoped for concerted, directed change). Whatever the reason for Lysenko's naïve attempt to rehabilitate Lamarck, the result was total disaster for both the grain and Soviet genetics: neither grew.

Can genes learn?

The bizarre history continues: in 1974 an American immunologist, William Summerlin, admitted faking the success of a skin graft on a mouse so as to convince colleagues that immune rejection of foreign tissues can, under certain circumstances, be avoided. Although not directly testing Lamarckian inheritance, Summerlin's work bears a strong affinity with Steele's and he appears to have sought success for a similar reason: both were convinced that the existing explanation of the immune response was inadequate.

Perhaps the most ironic aspect of this dossier is that it is far from certain that the researches of this supposed rogues' gallery were mistaken. As I mentioned, some of Kammerer's results using the sea squirt *Ciona* look convincingly Lamarckian. They have never been repeated. McDougall's rat experiments are still in need of a good explanation as they have been repeated. Also, recent immunological research has suggested that Summerlin need not have bothered to fake his results: he seems to have been right anyway. Whatever the ultimate truth about these Lamarckian loners, the story remains a fascinating case history in the sociology of science. Clearly, something deeper than an objective search for truth lies behind it. People want Lamarck to be right.

Certainly one reason for backing Lamarck is that his is a simpler explanation of the evolutionary process than the neo-Darwinian one. According to Occam's razor—which states that if faced with two conflicting explanations for an event, we must take the simpler until it is proved inadequate—Lamarckism is the superior theory precisely because it is simpler. It is a single-step process: the organism responds to its environment directly. According to neo-Darwinism the organism must first await random mutation before, second, selection sifts out the helpful from the harmful. Although it may be able to acclimatize to the vagaries of the environment during its life, the organism is helpless in passing on this acclimatization to its offspring because its genes have not changed. Adaptation, in this view, can only arise by spontaneous and random genetic events which just so happen to help the bearer. The British anthropologist Gregory

The Descent of Darwin

Bateson has described the difficulty of explaining adaptation by this traditional mutation/selection theory:

> The hypothetical pre-giraffe with the mutant gene 'long neck' will need to modify not only its heart and circulatory system but also perhaps semicircular canals, its intervertebral discs, its postural reflexes, the ratio of length thickness of many muscles, its evasive tactics *vis-à-vis* predators, etc.
>
> Bateson, 1963

In other words if, say, five genetic mutations are actually necessary to accomplish a bodily adaptation (complete with co-ordination of nerve, muscle, bone, blood supply and so on), are we reasonably to expect *all five* to occur at the same time in the same creature? If not, what are the chances that one of these mutations alone will be of any use at all? This is the real trouble with the existing theory; if a creature must passively await random mutations in order to cope, is it realistic to expect all the mutations necessary to accomplish a useful change to occur concomitantly? Surely not. If, on the other hand, a creature can respond actively within its lifetime, and then pass some of this acquired 'learning' on to its offspring, would it not explain the co-ordination of response that creatures would require in order to respond effectively to an environmental change?

Put in this light Lamarckism sounds reasonable. Lamarckism *is* reasonable. But, as one historian of science, Stephen Jay Gould, has pointed out—in fact referring to Lamarckism—'the tyranny of what seems reasonable often impedes science'. There is a difference between being reasonable and being right.

The main reason that any suggestion of Lamarckism is bound to run against the orthodox evolutionary grain is that it is assumed to contradict the 'central dogma' of biology. This central dogma states that the sex cells of a creature are isolated from the body cells and hence any bodily change during life will not influence offspring. If, for instance, you were to lose your arm in an accident at the age of fifteen, you would not subsequently give birth to armless children. Your reproductive cells are in that way independent of your body.

Can genes learn?

(In the case of a lost arm, this independence is obviously beneficial.) Something the neo-Lamarckians constantly seem to overlook is that:

> In our hope for the best we forget that we are invoking a principle that also calls for the inheritance of the worst.
>
> *T.H. Morgan, 1915*

A more modern interpretation of this central dogma is to say that information, in the genetic sense, flows one way only—from DNA to RNA to protein. DNA is the hereditary material that, via the intermediary 'translator' RNA, creates and determines the building blocks of the body (i.e. the proteins). DNA is handed down from parent to offspring, and at fertilization the DNA of a creature is determined as the parental sex cells come together. Bodily proteins—and bodily changes—cannot influence the DNA and so the hereditary blueprint is fixed.

Lamarckism implies that the 'sex' and 'body' cells are no longer isolated, and that information may actually flow backwards from the body to the hereditary material, the DNA. In other words, if Lamarckism occurs the body can send a message back to the genes saying, in effect, 'change this bit of DNA'. Analogously, according to Darwinian wisdom a 'teacher' can only teach the same 'lessons'—whether right or wrong—throughout his life; according to Lamarck the teacher may be capable of 'updating' his lessons as his pupils grow up and return to tell him where he went wrong.

Is it possible for information to flow back to the genes? If so, how could it happen? If any Lamarckian results are found to hold up, these will be the crucial questions. Steele maintained that such a reverse flow of information is possible and invoked a benign virus—a microscopic 'bag' of genetic information—as the transporter. This neatly side-steps the difficulty of transgressing biology's central dogma, in the following way: there has not been a reverse flow of information from protein to RNA to DNA, but rather entire chunks of DNA are being transferred. Suppose a mutant cell appears in the body and proliferates because it is more successful than the normal cells in some way. If a virus was capable of swapping the crucial chunk of new cellular DNA for old in the sex cells, we would have the potential for Lamarckian evolution. The virus would pick up information from the body's DNA and convey it to the DNA of the sex cells, thus changing the hereditary material during the lifetime of the creature. The only dogma that has been contradicted is the old notion that body and sex cells are totally isolated from each other. The modern ideas of information flow are not violated.

It is another ironic twist to the tale that this part of the Lamarckian hypothesis—invoking a virus as a DNA transporter—which sounds so absurd and contrived, is one process that is actually known to occur.

Viruses are known to invade living cells and to carry genetic information from creature to creature. It has even been recently suggested that such viruses may parasitize the DNA of higher organisms, thus helping to account for 'selfish' genes. As Howard Temin, who first suggested such a role for viruses, has said:

> In extreme cases one could imagine that a product of protovirus evolution would infect the germ (reproductive) line, become integrated there, and thus affect progeny organisms.
>
> *Temin, 1971*

An intriguing example of how such a transfer might occur has recently surfaced; it involves an observation which, no matter how it is ultimately explained, is bound to throw a spanner into the evolutionary works.

It has been known for some years that in the roots of the soya plant there flows a red fluid containing a haemoglobin very like the oxygen-carrying haemoglobin of animals. The red colour is actually due to the iron (haem means iron) in the haemoglobin molecule. The similarity is striking: if you cut the soya root, red 'blood' oozes out, and in the soya, as in animals, the haemoglobin carries oxygen to the tissues. In 1981 the startling discovery was made that not only did this leghaemoglobin (legume haemoglobin) look and act like the animal counterpart, but the DNA coding for it is virtually identical to the corresponding gene in animals.

Considering that, so far as is known, there is no haemoglobin in any plants other than a few legumes such as the soya, there are really only two possibilities to explain its presence: either coincidence or 'horizontal' transfer from an animal. The similarity in structure, which is highly complex, seems far too close for a coincidence, but how could a plant pick up an animal gene? One possibility put forward by Dr Alec Jeffreys at Leicester University is that a virus might have carried the gene from an animal—perhaps decaying in the soil—and transferred the haemoglobin gene in its entirety to the soya's roots, there to become incorporated in the plant's DNA. This is not to imply that the virus has done this for the benefit of the soya or the animal; it might have been a passive transfer or possibly beneficial to the virus itself. The entire story is mere speculation, but who has a better explanation?

It is certain that, at least so far, the evidence for Lamarckism is slight and suspect. Even if Steele's experiments, or for that matter Kammerer's, are repeated successfully the fact remains that the laboratory conditions required to obtain even a marginal response are so extreme as to bear little relation to the lives of creatures in their natural environs. Even if such Lamarckian inheritance occurs, furthermore, it is bound to remain the exception rather than the rule because of the overwhelming evidence in support of conventional Mendelian inheritance.

There are, however, at least two senses in which the established genetic thinking—and the established neo-Darwinian thinking—has been unnecessarily narrow-minded and complacent.

T. H. Morgan, the leading American geneticist in the first half of this century, first drew the parallel between 'organic' and 'cultural' evolution. Organic evolution refers to the transformation of living creatures over time, while cultural evolution refers to the transformation and increasing complexity of man's culture with time. While cultural evolution is not really evolution at all in the Darwinian sense, it is nevertheless analogous and is patently Lamarckian in its mechanism. We *can* inherit the acquired social skills of our ancestors. For Isaac Newton trigonometry was the pinnacle of his university education in mathematics; today trigonometry is taught at A level, or even below, as a prerequisite for university entrance. Culturally we have inherited Newton's acquired knowledge. Even in the semi-organic/semi-cultural area of instinct and behaviour is it not easier to envisage 'inherited plans of action' than the abrupt, random appearance of some isolated trait? Several respected neo-Darwinists have conceded this point, suggesting that changes in behaviour that are learned may predispose an animal to certain mutations, so helping to speed up adaptation. So at least in terms of cultural evolution Lamarck was right. Can we blame the maligned Lamarck, and some of his disciples, for perhaps seeing a cultural metaphor in the natural world?

The second sense in which the neo-Darwinists are too narrow-minded concerns what is known—or rather, what is *not* known—about inheritance. Although Steele's results may be unrepeatable, there is no theoretical reason why his suggestion should be wrong. It is certainly conceivable that such transmission of characters might occur. The reflex reaction against his ideas—almost in principle—was too impulsive. The possibilities for horizontal transfer of genetic information via, for example, viruses, are real—the soya haemoglobin may be the result of such an event. While this is not necessarily Lamarckian, it is certainly not Mendelian.

Similarly, some of the very recent research into the newly discovered repetitive DNA sequences (such as Dover's work; see Chapter 5, p. 76-8) is revealing inconsistencies in the existing genetical theory. The rapidity with which the repeats appear to spread, not only within the DNA of a creature but throughout populations of creatures, is just not consistent with simple Mendelian laws. As these ubiquitous repeats are now considered to be possibly essential in determining species boundaries—in other words, crucial to the origin of species— the suggestion of non-Mendelian spread is quite a blow to orthodox hereditary theory.

In short, 'there are more things in heaven and earth . . .'

Can genes learn?

than are dreamed of in the simple, mechanistic model of inheritance suggested by Mendel and adopted wholesale by the neo-Darwinists. While the basic rules do seem to apply convincingly, there are exciting aspects of inheritance which contradict and broaden the old story.

Chapter 9

Can genes build bodies?

———————————————— ✺ ————————————————

Omnes ab ovo—From the egg comes everything.
                                        William Harvey, 1651

If evolutionary theory is pictured as a jigsaw puzzle in which the various components of nature, such as geology or genetics, must interlock, then by far the largest missing piece is developmental biology. Our understanding of the processes by which a single fertilized egg develops into different cells, and then tissues and organs, and finally into a complex integrated machine, is pitifully inadequate; development is a study still in its infancy. It is hardly surprising, therefore, that there is no accepted theory of development. Far from it, the very history of ideas about embryology and ontogeny (that is, the entire course of development from conception to death) is a catalogue of semi-mystical terms and inadequate theories.

Unfortunate as this gap in knowledge is for biology in general, it is a serious handicap for evolutionary theory in particular. Developmental biology is central to evolution because it bridges the chasm between two quite separate fields—genetics and 'whole-animal' biology. This is the no man's land between 'genotype' and 'phenotype', between the ingredients of a meal and the finished dish itself. Development is the recipe that converts a bag of genes into an elephant, a snail, or an oak tree. This gap in understanding is especially important in relation to the theory of natural selection because, although selection must act on phenotypes, on the 'finished products', the vast bulk of natural selection theory is based on genotypes, the 'ingredients'. The basis of Darwinian ideas is that creatures vary in their ability to compete and survive and reproduce. But the theory itself is usually expressed in terms of the *genes* that are assumed to underlie all aspects of the creatures. The problem is that, so far, we have no coherent picture of how genes turn into creatures, of how genotypes become phenotypes. And until the exact relationship between genes and 'phenes' is known, evolutionary theory will remain speculative and untestable.

> Population geneticists, in their enthusiasm to deal with the changes in genotype frequencies that underlie evolutionary changes, have often forgotten that what are ultimately to be explained are the myriad and subtle changes in size, shape, behaviour, and interactions with other species that constitute the real stuff of evolution.
>
> *Lewontin, 1974*

Development is the missing link between these two elements. So what is development?

A fertilized egg is a single cell. Even a relatively simple creature such as a snail is comprised of hundreds of millions of cells differentiated into dozens of cell-types having different functions; liver cells, muscle cells, or brain cells. Development is a word to describe the processes whereby one cell becomes millions of cells all acting in an integrated and co-ordinated way. In the beginning the single cell divides into two, then four, then eight cells, still undifferentiated. Eventually this expanding tennis ball of cells begins to change shape, to turn inside out or squash itself in on one side. Then differences between cells become apparent and regions begin to assume a character of their own. These regions mark the beginnings of future bones and guts, muscles and nerves (see fig. 12).

At early stages the embryos of many animals look alike; a two-week old salamander is almost indistinguishable from a two-week old chicken or human being. As development proceeds, the embryo differentiates more and more into cell types and bodily structures, and the features that in adult life will enable instant recognition of 'type' become more apparent. The normal development of a given creature

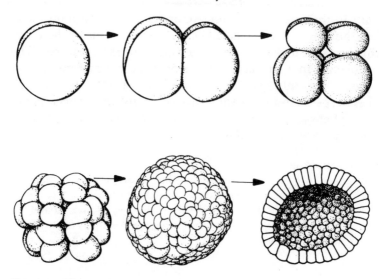

Fig. 12. The early stages of embryo formation. As the cells multiply, the embryo assumes different shapes. (After Cerfontaine and Conklin)

always follows the same path, and that path is remarkably stable and resistant to external conditions. Even a quite serious disruption, such as injury, can be overcome and repaired so long as it occurs at an early stage. So there is regularity in development as well as flexibility. Once set in motion, the processes by which an egg becomes an adult creature are hard to upset.

Where does the control of this process arise? A single cell eventually gives rise to millions of cells, each one playing a different role in the body. This 'production line' for life is incredibly complex and ordered; so where are the instructions? How does a particular cell know whether to become a muscle cell or a bone cell? What determines the intricate folding and unfolding in the embryo? Where is the 'blueprint' for bodily design, if there is one?

Although there is an extensive literature of descriptive embryology going back to the Greeks, not one of these key theoretical questions has yet been answered convincingly,

130

and these are the questions of interest to evolution. If an understanding of cell differentiation is the key to development, then we must discover the key to differentiation. Are the genes sufficient as a blueprint for building bodies? That is the question.

Lewis Wolpert is the leading British developmental biologist, and he has made a significant contribution to the understanding of growth. If you compare a man and a chimpanzee, says Wolpert, they appear quite different; and yet they possess *all* the same basic ingredients in terms of cell-types. Each has about 200 types of cell—the same ones. The only difference is that their spatial organization is different, the rules governing which cells have become nerve, muscle, or bone are different. If we could discover what tells a cell to become bone, or muscle, we would have gone some way towards an understanding of development. Wolpert has proposed a model for spatial organization based upon the *position* of each cell.

Imagine a French flag composed of red, white and blue vertical stripes. How could a 'cell'—some tiny part—of the flag know which colour to become in an 'embryonic' flag? One way would be if colour were determined by position. Suppose a substance, X, is secreted at the left-hand side of the flag. Its concentration will decrease gradually with distance from the source of secretion, from left to right. If 'cells' of the flag had sensitivity to this substance X, then depending upon the concentration of X a cell could interpret its position and become red, white or blue. So a cell that was programmed to respond to high levels of X would become blue, while one programmed to respond to lower levels would become white and so on. Through threshold concentrations acting as switches on the cells, a French flag would result (see fig. 13).

A crude example of 'positional information' from nature is found in Siamese cats. Siamese cats have generally pale-coloured coats except that their extremities are dark—the paws, the ear-tips, and the tail. These are also the coldest parts of a cat's anatomy and this, it transpires, is no coincidence. The pale colour results from a pigment which is synthesized only above a threshold temperature (which is

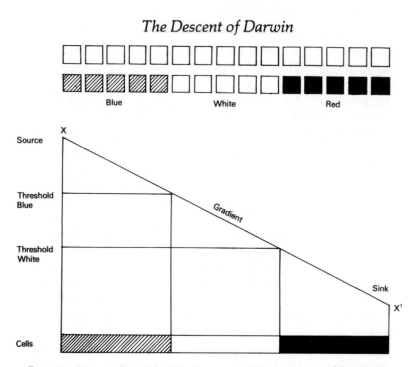

Fig. 13. How a line of cells that can differentiate as blue, white or red can be organized to form the French flag. Positional information is delivered by a gradient of a diffusible chemical. The top row represents undifferentiated cells.

roughly the cat's body temperature). The cat's extremities never reach this threshold temperature and so become dark because the pale pigment is never synthesized. Position has determined colour.

Wolpert's positional information theory seems incredibly crude to account for the complex, three-dimensional processes of embryonic change, and yet it remains the best approach that developmental biologists have come up with so far. The idea is that chemical activators diffuse through embryonic tissues, thereby 'informing' the cells of their whereabouts. The cells are programmed—genetically—to respond in different ways to the chemical concentrations, and this, to pursue the flag analogy, results in cells becoming red, white or blue. The cells know what to become by 'reading off' the chemicals around them. The genes of a creature are programmed so that for a particular combination of chemicals, each cell knows whether to become nerve, or bone, or brain.

Various intricate experiments have been performed to test this idea, and so far the results have been cautiously convincing. For example, a transplanted cell or group of cells behaves as one would expect if it were interpreting position—an embryonic red 'cell' transplanted to the blue stripe will become blue and vice versa. As Wolpert has said, there is now '. . . substantial evidence that gradients in positional information underlie pattern formation in a variety of organisms'.

The trouble with this theory is that it only really puts back the important question by one step. If cells can interpret their positions, how do they do it? Is this genetically determined? What are the chemicals responsible for carrying such information? How can cells record and remember their position? Wolpert believes that the underlying programme is genetic, that genes determine the activating chemicals and, similarly, that genes interpret position. He is convinced that development is programmed by the genes, so that they provide not only the building blocks for the body but also the instructions for putting them together. Although he is happy to admit that our present understanding of genetics is inadequate to explain development (he has said that 'the logic of the genome remains a closed book'), it is in this direction that he seeks a solution.

Although this straightforward explanation is consistent with observation, there is a strong feeling among many developmental biologists that there is more to embryology than positional information alone. For one thing the basic properties of development, such as regulation and flexibility, are also seen in unicellular creatures. Since in Wolpert's view the cell is the basic unit of development, this is a definite drawback to his interpretation, suggesting that the underlying cause cannot be single cells reading off positions. Why does one see the same reading off *within* a single-celled creature?

Another drawback to Wolpert's ideas is that genetic

determination of development implies an inflexibility which one does not find in nature. When a bone, such as the femur, is broken accidentally during an animal's lifetime, it frequently reforms in an abnormal fashion. The bone cells, as well as the attached muscles, nerves, and tendons, can often regrow to accommodate the change so as to produce a slightly different—though fully functional—leg structure. But how do the cells 'know' how to accommodate and reposition themselves to produce the new leg? Surely if position is the key to development, and genes are the key to position, such plasticity would not be found? After all, the genes are assumed not to change during life, so how can their messages change?

The transformations of the embryo, the extraordinary repeatability within a species, the plasticity to overcome perturbations, all these help to create a sense of almost mystic awe at the phenomenon. Cut a flatworm into three and each part will regenerate into whole flatworms; remove the lens from a newt's eye and the surrounding tissue will grow a new lens (see fig. 14); chop the leg off an insect and it will regenerate a new leg. It is certainly hard to imagine that genes alone have the ability to fulfil all these functions—of being the building blocks, of being also the instructions for putting

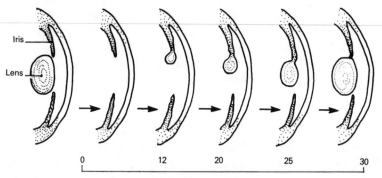

Days after surgical removal of lens

Fig. 14. Regeneration of a lens from the margin of the iris in a newt's eye after the surgical removal of the original lens. (After Needham, 1942)

the blocks together, *and* of being capable of regenerating lost parts and repairing damage. It is almost as if the organism had a unity, an integrity, beyond the reducible parts that comprise it.

This integrity is bound to jar with the reductionist neo-Darwinism which is constantly trying to explain the whole in terms of the machine-like interaction of simple components. According to neo-Darwinism genes *are* ultimately capable of building, programming and repairing bones; similarly selection *is* capable of changing, over many generations, individual genes to enhance survival. All gradations of form are, therefore, theoretically possible, and it should be feasible to tinker with single parts of a body to change aspects here and there at will. But the observations of nature don't suggest this at all. Rather we are struck by the unity and integrity of whole organisms, and their resistance to change, *despite* the outside world. Also changes don't appear to happen piecemeal; they seem to occur in co-ordinated ways that defy explanation in terms of single, step-like changes.

Take an example from motor cars. Car engines are ridiculously simple in comparison with the complex interactions of the most primitive creatures, yet is it possible to alter a single aspect of that motor without also changing other aspects? Even the smallest alteration in some feature— lengthening the piston rods, narrowing the cylinders, changing the spark-plug timing—may actually damage the motor unless accompanied by other co-ordinated responses.

The common lesson in all this is that organisms are not pieces of putty, infinitely moldable by infinitesimal degrees in any direction, but are, rather, complex and resilient structures endowed with innumerable constraints and opportunities . . . Organic integrity always received lip service, but in a subtle, yet pervasive way, the strict Darwinism of recent times has encouraged us to put this truth on the back shelf and to consider development primarily as a source for the unconstrained, small, random variants that provide raw material only and make natural selection the sole directing force in evolution. And this subtle emphasis explains why so many fine embryologists, from Berrill to Waddington, were never comfortable with the modern synthesis.

Gould, 1981

This apparent incompatibility between neo-Darwinism and embryology is best illustrated by the idea of 'constraints' proposed by Gould (see also Chapter 4, p. 52-5). If one looks at cell-types, or organs, or even whole creatures, they fall into definite categories. There are muscle cells, nerve cells and bone cells; there are hearts, brains and femurs; cats, dogs and mice. This implies, since there are not intermediates, that not all types of cell, or organ, are possible—that of all the possible varieties that could exist, only some do exist. Why should this be? Why are there no cells intermediate between, say, skin or muscle; why are there no organs intermediate between heart and brain?

According to neo-Darwinism such spaces or gaps could only exist because they are non-adaptive, because natural selection has eliminated such variants. In other words, all variants are possible, but only a small proportion enhance the functioning of the creature and these are the cell-types, organs, or species which we see around us. But another possible explanation is gaining credibility among developmental biologists which suggests that all variants are *not* possible, that the spaces exist because of 'constraints' on development.

What is a constraint? It is a limiting influence on possible pathways, a force which restricts the outcome of a given process. In developmental terms, could it be that the explanation for these spaces is that these forms simply could not exist because of the physical or chemical laws governing growth? As an example, take a light switch on a wall; most switches are of the 'on-off' variety so that as you push the lever from 'on' to 'off' there is a sudden jump as the switch changes mode. Such a switch has a limited set of positions at the two extremes; there is no stable intermediate position. So it is not as if all these intermediates once existed and were eliminated by choice. The very design of the switch means that the intermediates *cannot* exist.

Can genes build bodies?

Looking at engines again as an analogy: imagine that one wanted to increase the power of a vehicle from a few horsepower to thousands of pounds of thrust. At the lower end of the scale a simple motor-cycle's two-stroke motor is most efficient, but as one increases the power requirement the best motor becomes a four-stoke with six or eight cylinders. More power still requires abandoning the internal combustion engine and building a turbine with rotary blades; NASA's rockets are different again—powered by high-energy fuels with almost no moving parts. The important point is that there are no intermediates between these engines. There is no gradual transition from two-stroke to turbine. The different engines were designed for different functions and there is no way that tinkering with a two-stroke would eventually give you a moon-rocket—they have totally different start- and end-points. Once you have started to build a turbine, your possibilities are severely constrained by the laws of metallurgy, and of chemistry and physics.

The idea that development might be canalized into definite pathways determined by the physical laws of construction and design was proposed in the 1930s by the great C.H. Waddington. Waddington coined the term 'epigenetic landscape', by which he envisaged development as analogous to movement through a hilly landscape. A ball rolling through it will only be able to take a limited number of paths because of the hills and valleys (see figs. 15 and 16).

The importance of this metaphor is that it enables one to visualize two important elements of development: the regularity and the flexibility. Any ball set in motion at the same point on the landscape will end up in the same place. Thus the terrain determines the end-point and this end-point will be repeatedly reached. At the same time the system is resistant to small perturbations. If you were to shift the ball slightly while it rolled down a steep-sided valley, it would rapidly resume its normal position because gravity would pull it back. The ball, therefore, does not have a limitless freedom to travel wherever it wishes over the terrain; its path is narrowly constrained by the landscape. Only a strong disturbance will change its course. At some points, of course,

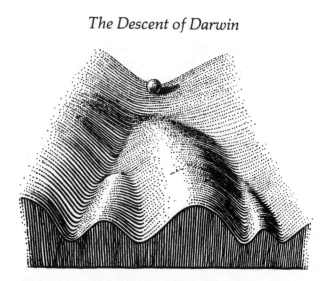

Fig. 15. Part of an epigenetic landscape. The hills and valleys are developmental constraints that allow the ball to take only a limited number of paths. (After Waddington, 1957)

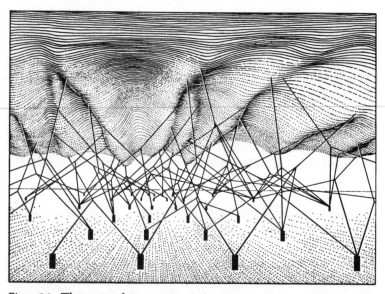

Fig. 16. The complex system of interactions underlying the epigenetic landscape. The genes in effect act like guy-ropes to model it. (After Waddington, 1957)

the force required to change course may be quite small; at a valley head where there is a split, a slight push could be all that makes the difference between rolling down one valley or the next. Could this be the sort of event leading to the differentiation of male and female, or muscle cell and brain cell?

The epigenetic landscape is a useful conceptual tool in trying to understand development because it helps one to envisage the properties of regulation, plasticity and constraint. According to Waddington the landscape is determined directly by genes, the interaction of gene products determining the hills and valleys of growth, and at the same time the limitations and the possibilities of development. The constraints are therefore parts of the landscape which are not traversable because of the physical and chemical properties of the developing embryo. This is important because it implies that natural selection may be largely irrelevant in development. The 'spaces' of form which one never finds have not been weeded out by selection; they simply could not exist. All possible types (of cell, of tissue, of species) are not equally likely—many could never exist because of the physical and chemical laws of growth. Granted, selection may weed out the unfit, but it is not responsible for determining the fit, nor is it responsible for the range of possibilities that are available. And that is a profound change of emphasis for neo-Darwinism which imagines the environment as the sole judge of fitness in an infinite field of possibilities.

So the idea of constraints envisaged by Waddington turns out to challenge the supremacy of selection. It is an idea now receiving a lot of attention from developmental biologists. Some of them believe that the study of the forces limiting biological structure may prove vital to evolutionary theory.

A few have gone a step further and questioned the very foundation of development: genetics. Brian Goodwin from Sussex University, for example, is not at all convinced by Wolpert's ideas of positional information, and the implied genetic basis of development. It was Goodwin who first pointed out that the pattern formation which Wolpert describes in complex creatures, such as chicks or mice, is also found in unicellular creatures (see p. 133). How, he argues, can the basic unit of development be the cell, as Wolpert maintains? Surely it must be something smaller. Goodwin also points out that the way in which parts of a creature can be regenerated is incompatible with simple positional theories. If you cut a slice off an invertebrate such as *Hydra*, that slice will regenerate the entire organism, but at a reduced size. The pattern is the same, but the scale is different. How could positional theory account for this?

The criticisms are valid; Wolpert admits the limitations of his ideas to multicellular creatures, and doesn't pretend to explain the 'microscopic molecular' interactions. But Goodwin goes beyond this criticism to propose an alternative explanation: *fields* rather than *genes*. Goodwin believes that the genes could not provide both the ingredients and the recipe for development. The genes may be the basic building blocks of life but the recipe or the programme for development arises from 'morphogenetic fields', rather like electric or magnetic fields, which order the proteins. In other words just as a magnet can order iron filings into lines and curves, could a morphogenetic field be responsible for ordering the proteins made by genes? There are some tantalizing observations which appear to support these ideas. Intricate mathematical equations (which are known to be useful in predicting the behaviour of magnetic or electric fields) do appear to predict some aspects of development which are inexplicable otherwise. Field constancy, for example, the integrated response in a way analogous to that seen in simple unicellular creatures.

> This is why organisms cannot be reduced to their genes, since the latter determine only the *potential* composition of the organism, not its form. This does not deny that composition can influence or constrain form; only that it is not in general sufficient to determine it.
>
> *Goodwin, 1978*

Goodwin's approach to development has grown into a vehement denial of neo-Darwinism with its reductionist,

Can genes build bodies?

'genes-determine-all' approach. One can sympathize with his doubts that simple positional information theory will explain the complex and integrated transformations in development. But Goodwin has really gone too far; he appears to have been engulfed in a sort of neo-Pythagorean mysticism, a mathematical romanticism, which denies genes and even denies evolution:

> All organisms, then, are fields of the same generic type and it is this property which defines the living domain, not historical descendance from a hypothetical common ancestral type.
>
> *Goodwin, 1978*

This denial of genes and history, and reliance upon integrated wholes and mathematics, is intriguing, but the trouble is that Goodwin is not talking the same language as other biologists. Neither is he backing up his revolutionary proposals with experiments. His is really a structuralist philosophical attack. It is a pity he is not turning it into hard science, because the intuitive appeal of his refreshing approach is strong.

The same criticism can be levelled at another recent revolutionary reappraisal of development by the now infamous Rupert Sheldrake. Sheldrake's book, *A New Science of Life*, published in 1981, was greeted by the scientific community with incredulity. Many scientific journals had difficulty finding anyone who would review the book. This was largely because Sheldrake—a botanist of high scientific repute—had proposed a completely alternative interpretation of the origins of biological form and structure.

According to Sheldrake, form in nature (both organic and inorganic) is determined by morphogenetic fields, rather like Goodwin's fields, except that these fields are able to influence other fields in both space and time:

> This influence could even involve an 'action at a distance' in both space *and time* of a type not yet recognised by physics.
>
> *Sheldrake, 1981*

Sheldrake's radical idea is that things are the way they are because of a sort of habit—because that is the way their predecessors were. Form is determined by fields from

141

previous form. By this argument the genes are once more reduced to building blocks, and the recipe which puts them together is an ethereal field that is passed on at the same time as the genes. Sheldrake's fields are very like Goodwin's, with the added component that they are heritable (in a non-genetic way) and capable of influencing other fields.

To illustrate this idea Sheldrake has a very elegant and droll metaphor. Imagine, he says, a Martian coming to earth and seeing a television for the first time:

> He might at first suppose that the set actually contained little people, whose images he saw on the screen. But when he looked inside and found only wires, condensers, transistors etc., he might adopt the more sophisticated hypothesis that the images somehow arose from complicated interactions among the components of the set. This hypothesis would seem particularly plausible when he found that the images became distorted or disappeared completely when components were removed, and that the images were restored to normal when these components were put back in their proper places. If the suggestion was put to him that the images in fact depended on invisible influences entering the set from far away, he might reject it on the grounds that it was unnecessary and obscurantist.
>
> *Sheldrake, 1981*

Outrageous as the idea sounds (and it is pretty far-fetched), Sheldrake claims indirect evidence to support his hypothesis from several sources including chemistry, physics, and animal behaviour. The most striking support comes from a series of experiments which were carried out in the 1930s and 1940s by the eminent American biologist William McDougall. McDougall (whose work was referred to in Chapter 8, p. 119) set up a water puzzle for rats and found that the ability to tackle the puzzle successfully improved from generation to generation (in the absence of selection). More significantly, when other workers attempted to repeat his work they found that the *first* generation of rats they used—which were totally unrelated to McDougall's rats— were able to tackle the puzzle as successfully as the *last* generation of McDougall's rats. Were they inherently cleverer rats? Or had they, as Sheldrake now claims, actually 'inherited' the ability through a trans-spatial and trans-temporal morphogenetic field? Sheldrake's interpretation is that the learning of McDougall's rats had become incorporated into the rats' 'fields' and thus, presumably, *all* rats *everywhere* suddenly acquired the ability to tackle such a puzzle more successfully. It sounds fantastic. What lends a certain credibility to the ideas, however, is that first, for some phenomena (such as McDougall's researches) there is no convincing alternative explanation and second, Sheldrake claims that his hypothesis is testable.

Many scientists—including Lewis Wolpert—have been very rude about Sheldrake's book. It has been called 'arrant nonsense' and, by an editorial in *Nature*, a prime 'candidate for burning'. The most generous thing to say about Sheldrake's ideas is that they are intriguing but sorely in need of scientific experimentation. Of course, Sheldrake is caught in a 'catch-22' so far as research is concerned; with respectable scientists calling his book ridiculous he is unlikely to get funds from any research council to test the theory. Yet how can he establish the theory without research? This vicious circle of science applies to many of the controversial ideas now being proposed—a sort of scientific version of 'the rich get richer and the poor get poorer'.

It is clear that the shroud of semi-mysticism which has hung about developmental biology is still there, presumably because there is so little verifiable theory to account for the observations. Although both Goodwin and Sheldrake have pointed out anomalies in the existing ideas, and have suggested lines of research which would be profitable for *any* developmental biologist, they both appear to have plunged into the deep end with their theories. In Goodwin's case one suspects that his structuralist philosophy is playing too important a role compared with experiment and observation. Similarly for Sheldrake, although he seems to have gone back virtually to vitalism in an attempt to explain the incredible complexity of development. As was said in a totally different context: 'C'est magnifique, mais ce n'est pas la guerre!' It's fascinating, but it isn't really science.

The Descent of Darwin

One man who does appear to have struck a more reasonable note in the debate about reductionist versus non-reductionist ideas of development is Gunther Stent. Stent commands the respect of the scientific community—he is an accomplished biologist and theoretician—yet he has recently denied that genes could be considered as incorporating a programme for development:

> In this regard the genetic approach to development resembles the quantum mechanical approach to genetics that had some vogue in the '30s and '40s.
>
> *Stent, 1981*

Stent thinks that the hope of explaining development in terms of genes is as naïve as the hope—current in the 1930s and 1940s—of explaining genes in terms of atoms. Although genes are made up of countless atoms and their complex interconnections, to begin to explain heredity in terms of chemical bonds is naïvely mechanistic, and of course it never worked.

Similarly, says Stent, the current belief that the key to development lies in a genetic programme may be simplistic and naïve. Besides, the notion of a programme implies a pre-ordained rigidity which is a far cry from the actual flexibility of development. The fact that embryo growth is regular and predictable (within limits) does not mean that it is programmatic. To illustrate the distinction between programmed and non-programmed events, Stent uses the analogy of a performance of *Hamlet.* If one goes to the theatre to see *Hamlet* one is witnessing two distinct types of event: the performance itself, which is programmatic, since there is a direct one-to-one correspondence with the written play, and the various concomitants of the performance, such as the finding of seats, the curtain rising, the interval drinks and so on. These events are as much a part of the play as Shakespeare's writing, but they are in no sense programmed. They are regular and predictable, but not programmatic. Might the same apply to genes in their relation to development?

144

Can genes build bodies?

The fact that mutation of a gene leads to an altered phenotype shows that genes are part of the causal antecedents of the adult organism, but does not in any way indicate that the mutant gene is part of a programme for development.

Stent, 1981

In other words, genes may be an essential part of development but they are not necessarily the *cause* of the regularity. Development might be a historical rather than a programmed process in the sense that once the chain of events has been set in motion, the unfolding may happen by itself, or as Stent puts it 'one thing simply leads to another'. If you put a pot containing oil and popcorn onto a cooker and turn the dial to its hottest, and come back in two hours, you will undoubtedly find popcorn and oil all over your kitchen. Now you would not find this if you forgot to turn the heat on, or if you didn't put the corn into the pot in the beginning. So each of these things (oil, corn, pot, heat) is necessary for the result, but the result was not programmed anywhere; it was simply an inevitable outcome of the starting conditions.

A good example of such a historical process is the establishment of ecological communities on newly formed islands. The appearance of 'virgin' islands (after, say, a volcanic eruption) is followed by a regular and predictable series of colonizations (as simple and then more complex organisms are able to exploit the resources) generally leading to—in similar parts of the world—very similar communities of plants and animals. There may be variations in the exact order of colonization, or the length of time taken, but the finished product is remarkably constant. So, given similar starting conditions, one thing leads to another in a regular, yet flexible, way that is clearly not programmed. Could development be such a process?

Stent's proposal is that the genes of the fertilized egg provide the starting conditions for embryo-formation, but that the complex events of development follow one from another rather than being pre-ordained or programmed into the genome. This is an attractive half-way house between the somewhat blinkered reductionism of Wolpert and the semi-mystic field equations of Goodwin or Sheldrake. It also lifts

145

the awesome responsibility for both 'ingredients' and 'recipe' from the genome, leaving it with the role of 'building blocks', which is, after all, the only *known* role of genes. That is not to say that there are not genes responsible for influencing crucial events of development, just that such genes were not 'programmed' to act in that way. To a geneticist this distinction may seem like splitting hairs, but it isn't: it may be an important shift in the way biologists think about development.

It is rather like looking at some optical illusions. One minute you see one pattern, the next minute you see another. The colours and forms have not moved, just your impression of what they represent (see fig. 17).

It is clear that an understanding of development—when it is finally attained—is going to be important for evolutionary theory. The neo-Darwinists think that natural selection is able to mould creatures piecemeal to create virtually any end-product; a growing knowledge of developmental constraints may suggest that this is not true, that the range of possibilities may be quite strictly limited. The neo-Darwinists envisage the genes as both the ingredients *and* the recipe for life; an appreciation of development may show that the role of genes has been overrated, that they are not a programme after all. There is one more aspect of development which remains relatively unexplained but which potentially might have a profound influence upon evolutionary theory. This is the notion that changes in developmental timing might be a source of dramatic new variants.

At the end of the last century Ernst Haeckel made the bold proposal that 'ontogeny recapitulates phylogeny'. What this tongue-twisting motto really means is that during the course of development a creature ascends its own evolutionary lineage, so that the various forms of the embryo represent past ancestors of that creature. One can see superficially what Haeckel had in mind; a human embryo looks decidedly fish-like at one stage (it even has gill pouches at this time) and only begins to resemble a human towards the end of gestation. Also, closely related creatures—those assumed to have had common ancestry until recent times—such as a pig and man,

146

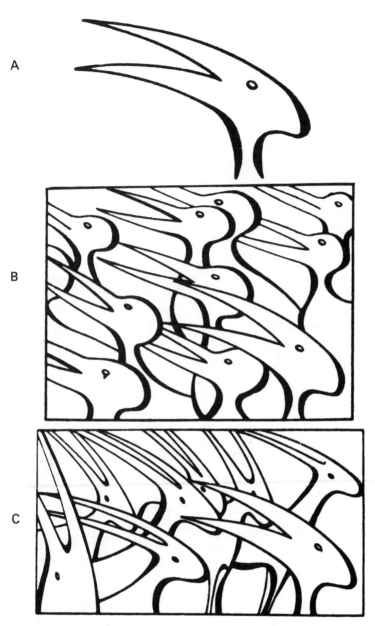

Fig. 17. What is A? Against a background of ducks (B) it is a duck, but against a background of antelopes (C) it becomes an antelope. Is this how we see facts against the background of a theory? (After Hanson, 1958)

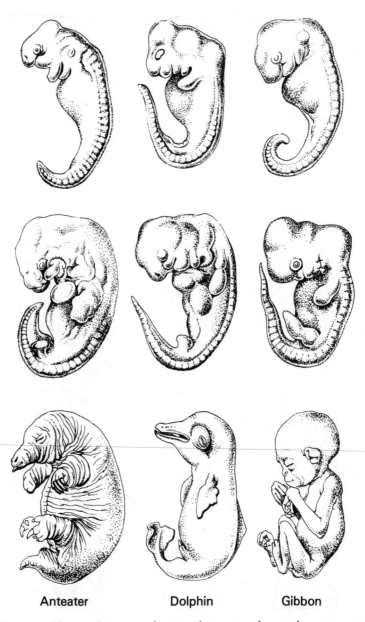

Anteater　　　　**Dolphin**　　　　**Gibbon**

Fig. 18. The striking similarities between the early stages of vertebrates led Haeckel to believe that an embryo ascends its own evolutionary lineage. Why does a gibbon (or even a human) embryo go through a gill pouch stage?

have virtually identical embryos in the initial states; it is only at the later stages that the differences become apparent (see fig. 18).

Haeckel is now known to have been mistaken. Although a study of embryology can provide vital clues to ancestry or relationship, it is now realized that the early stages of an embryo do not actually represent ancestral forms; rather it could be said that embryonic development 'betrays' ancestry since developmental pathways are not lightly discarded once evolved. In other words, one would expect the horse and the zebra to have similar paths of development since they are so closely related. That is not to say that the zebra evolved into the horse or vice versa, just that their long-shared ancestry (until they diverged) is bound to be reflected in development.

However, the dramatic changes of form that occur during ontogeny—just look at a frog's metamorphosis—raise an intriguing possibility (which was briefly discussed in Chapter 5). What would happen if sexual maturity were reached, or development were to stop, at an earlier or later stage than is normal? In fact this is known to occur in the South American newt, the axolotl. The axolotl goes through a metamorphosis from a tadpole stage (with gill slits and external gills) to a terrestrial stage (with lungs, and no external gills) rather like the common frog. Sexual maturity is normally reached in the terrestrial form, but occasionally the aquatic form reaches sexual maturity, *and never goes on to metamorphose*. This 'neoteny', the attainment of sexual maturity by a juvenile form, caused considerable confusion among early naturalists who thought that the axolotl was actually two separate species. And that is the point. By attaining an early sexual maturity development has been arrested and a new creature has been 'created'. In this way major changes in form can be accomplished without the need for genetic upheavals—since the genetic structure of the creatures is the same.

Stephen Jay Gould has pioneered the recent renewal of interest in such phenomena otherwise neglected since Haeckel's day. Gould actually points to man as a classic case of neoteny. If one compares human development with that of, say, a chimpanzee, there is a distinct similarity between

149

the *adult* human and the *juvenile* chimp. Size and shape of the head, and the hair distribution, are the same (hair being restricted to head, armpits, and groin). Yet the adult chimp looks quite different—it has a markedly 'ape-like' skull shape and pervasive hairiness. Could it be, argues Gould, that the transition from ape-like ancestor to man was accomplished, not by the piecemeal selection of individual traits such as skull shape, lack of hair and so on, but rather by a simple change in developmental timing? If sexual maturity was reached at progressively earlier stages could not man have evolved from his ancestors without any significant genetic alteration? Might man be a sort of promiscuous ape—one that attains sexuality before physical maturity? The possibility is intriguing and convincing because it explains not only the remarkable similarity between a young ape and adult man, it also explains why these close relatives have a virtually identical genetic make-up to our own (less than 1 per cent difference).

Again one can sense that a better understanding of development may open up locked rooms full of new possibilities and explanations. Development may help to explain the origin of new forms and may shift the emphasis away from genetics when it comes to explaining how these new forms arise. In several ways the neo-Darwinist world could change dramatically if the ideas of Goodwin, Stent or Gould were found to hold up. But, as I mentioned at the start of the chapter, the study of development is still in its infancy. It will undoubtedly give a rich yield when it is mined effectively, but for the time being we must steer clear of some of the more mystical theorizing and await some concrete results.

Chapter 10

A loss of confidence in Darwin?

———————————— ✸ ————————————

What are we to make of these current doubts about Darwinism?

Is Darwinism a scientific theory? It is not falsifiable in the strict Popperian sense, but it is testable and therefore scientific. The idea of 'survival of the fittest' can be—and often is—used tautologously, and this is something the neo-Darwinists must avoid if the theory is actually to explain observations from nature.

How strong is natural selection? In short, not as strong as many neo-Darwinists seem to assume. First of all it is very difficult to pin down and measure effectively. Second, although it is possible to demonstrate strong selection in artificial conditions can we be sure that such selection takes place in the wild? Many of the observations of variation and selection in nature suggest that it may not be very strong at all.

How do new species arise? By a variety of means, it would appear. While there is strong evidence for the classic neo-Darwinian mechanism of isolation plus selection leading to new species, the story is now thought to be much more complex than this. Recent work has emphasized the importance of fairly abrupt large-scale genetic events (such as polyploidy, or chromosome changes, or Dover's 'concerted' evolution) in speciation, and this certainly undermines the implied gradualism of neo-Darwinism.

Why don't we see gradual transition in the fossils? The fact is that we do not see gradualism in vast chunks of the fossil

151

record; this may be because of the very nature of the imperfect record (as Darwin believed) or it may actually reflect the reality of change. Such 'punctuationism' need not contradict the ideas of neo-Darwinism but it certainly implies that, once again, an understanding of evolution requires more than the population geneticists can predict or explain at present.

Can we separate pattern from process? It may be rather blinkered to do so, but have preconceived notions of process up to now biased our observations of the pattern? The cladists think that much of the 'filling in the gaps' in evolutionary history has been unfounded story-telling, and that the idea of ancestry is very difficult to treat scientifically. From their point of view neo-Darwinism is not necessarily wrong, it is just largely irrelevant to their work.

Can genes learn from experience? Apparently not, but they can do a lot of things which Mendel never dreamed of. Recent attempts to revive Lamarck's ideas appear to have failed, even if there are some tantalizing experiments still to be repeated. News that genes may be 'driven' rapidly through genomes and populations, and the bizarre possibility that certain genes may have been 'transplanted' from one species to another in the past, certainly widen the genetic horizons. Such events, if they do happen at all frequently, are bound to cause a rethink of some basic neo-Darwinian principles.

Are genes sufficient as a blueprint for development? Nobody knows, but a significant number of developmental biologists doubt if they are. This field is wide open at the present, but it is certain that when a coherent theory of development emerges it will throw much-needed light on the mechanism of evolution. At the moment the semi-mystical 'field' theories are scientifically weak, but there are growing doubts that the genes alone contain the 'programme' for development.

*   *   *

A loss of confidence?

Although several aspects of neo-Darwinism are being thoroughly criticized, and despite recent research suggesting that there are embarrassing gaps in the theory, very few biologists are abandoning ship. Even many of the most active critics—such as Gould and Lewontin—are fundamentally still neo-Darwinists who seek modifications to the basic principles; they are loathe to throw out an imperfect story while there is no coherent alternative. Others, such as Goodwin and Sheldrake, appear to have crossed a semi-mystical threshold into a world with a different framework altogether. A few, such as Patterson, simply maintain that neo-Darwinism is not necessarily right or wrong, but irrelevant to good biology. Many biologists are largely unaware that the attacks are as widespread as they are. Generally, however, there is not one biologist in a thousand who denies the neo-Darwinian synthesis of evolutionary theory.

Nevertheless there is no smoke without fire. When leading biologists start writing articles for scientific journals entitled *Is a New Evolutionary Synthesis Necessary?* (Stebbins and Ayala, 1981), or *In Defence of neo-Darwinism* (Charlesworth, Lande and Slatkin, 1982), or *Is a New and General Theory of Evolution Emerging?* (S. J. Gould, 1980), we can be sure that, regardless of the outcome, a lively debate is at hand. Can the neo-Darwinists salvage their theory by stipulating *ad hoc* caveats and modifications? Or are we on the verge of a new, more general theory?

In the popular mind there is still a confusion between evolutionism and Darwinism; if you were to tell the man 'on the Clapham omnibus' that there were doubts about Darwinism he would most likely interpret this as a rejection of evolution itself. This is the sort of misunderstanding that many creationists exploit to peddle their own anti-evolution. Of course this is mistaken. While Darwinism may stand or fall as a valid explanation for evolution, evolution itself is not in question; the evidence from geology alone is sufficient to reject any other interpretation.

What *is* in question is the confident, almost arrogant,

bravado of the neo-Darwinists in the 1940s, 1950s and 1960s. Here is Julian Huxley writing in 1953:

> The discovery of the principles of natural selection made evolution comprehensible; together with the discoveries of modern genetics, it has rendered all other explanations of evolution untenable.

Huxley, 1953

This is typical of the Darwinist at that time, yet it contrasts sharply with the Darwinian attitude now. Today, not even the most ardent supporter of neo-Darwinism would make such an unqualified claim to omniscience.

With the mushrooming growth in biology over the past twenty-five years has come an awareness that evolution entails more than Julian Huxley and his modern synthesis cohorts imagined. This healthy expansion of horizons—of which the attacks in this book are only the most recent manifestation—has led to a loss of arrogance among present-day neo-Darwinists compared to their omniscient predecessors of forty years ago.

This has partly arisen out of a sense of confusion. The tools at our disposal for unlocking the secrets of life seem so crude—rather like trying to eat a boiled egg with a pitchfork. At one level we see a gibbon swinging effortlessly from branch to branch, a machine incredibly well-designed for jungle survival (see fig. 19); yet when we try to grasp a closer understanding of one aspect of the gibbon's life—how and when does it reproduce? Is it variable for a particular enzyme gene? How did its musculature evolve from an ancestor?—we find that either it is virtually impossible to measure that aspect reliably, or else we are confronted with a vast collection of ambiguous evidence which eludes any simple interpretation.

A classic example of such difficulty can be seen in D'Arcy Thompson's analysis of structure using Cartesian coordinates (see figs. 20 and 21). D'Arcy Thompson showed that for many related creatures all the apparently distinct external differences between them could often be accounted for by a single integral transformation of coordinates. A human skull, for example (when seen superimposed upon a simple two-

Fig. 19. '. . . a machine incredibly well-designed for jungle survival.' The gibbon.

dimensional grid), can be easily transformed to resemble a very ape-like skull by changing a single aspect of one coordinate. This suggests that evolution itself may result from relatively simple coordinated change. Yet how do we begin to explain so many separate, yet integrated alterations in bones, nerves, muscles, life-style and so on, in terms of natural selection, or individually 'selfish' genes? In short, we cannot. In the case of both the gibbon and D'Arcy Thompson's coordinates, we see nature achieving simple, integrated results while the tools at our disposal are too crude to find out how she managed it.

As ever, Darwin himself was well aware of the difficulties in explaining the subtlety and holism of nature by his ideas, but he felt that this was more a difficulty of the imagination than one of reason. He had faith, in other words, that the discoveries of biology would vindicate natural selection, and that the puzzles of today would be explained tomorrow in

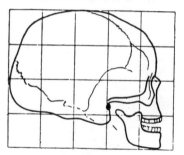

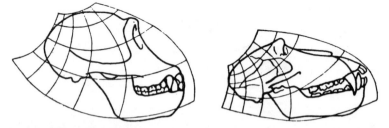

Fig. 20. D'Arcy Thompson projected the rectangular coordinates of a human skull (above) to produce a chimpanzee skull (below left) and a baboon skull (below right). (After Thompson, 1942)

terms of gradual selection. Of course, there is no reason to suppose that we should reject neo-Darwinism just because in 1982 it has trouble with a gibbon, or with D'Arcy Thompson's coordinates. The problem is not that Darwinian ideas are necessarily wrong—there are many good reasons why these ideas are right—but that there is much more to the story than the Darwinists can account for. Perhaps if we were to open our minds to new possibilities, to look at nature in different ways, we might be rewarded by some fresh insights.

Gabriel Dover's work on the 'horizontal' spread of genes, and the striking parallel between chromosome changes and species, must broaden the neo-Darwinian story of speciation. An appreciation of the extent of gene variation, and the apparently 'neutral' effect of most variants, must bring a reappraisal of the strength of selection in nature. The failure of neo-Darwinism to *predict* the patterns found in the fossil

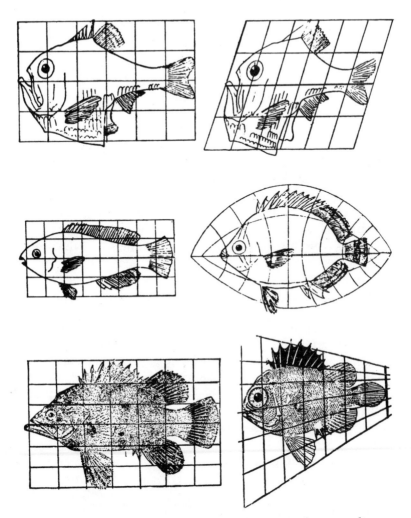

Fig. 21. A simple transformation of rectangular coordinates appears to 'explain' some complex species differences. How atomistic can natural selection be? (After Thompson, 1942)

record—in other words the fact that the neo-Darwinists seem to be able to 'explain' the fossil evidence no matter what it is—may mean that macroevolution is really a field in its own right, with its own observations and theories. The difficulties inherent in re-creating evolutionary history and determining ancestry must inhibit the penchant for 'story-telling' and the glib speculation. Why must the neo-Darwinists always try to open *all* the doors of nature with the same key? Is it not reasonable to assume that we may need more than one? If we continue to assume that one will suffice, are we not in danger of blinkering our vision?

There is another important reason for the loss of confidence in neo-Darwinism, and it really has nothing to do with neo-Darwinism or even with biology *per se*. Over the past few years there has grown a general loss of confidence in *all* science—a disenchantment with the reductionist approach, and an appreciation that science may not be quite as objective as the scientists would have us believe. A few examples from the history of biology will illustrate the point about objectivity.

The interpretations of the tempo of evolution have, as we have seen, varied enormously—from extreme catastrophism through punctuationism to out-and-out gradualism. But who have the main proponents of these interpretations been? The strongest advocate of pre-Darwinian catastrophism was Cuvier. Cuvier's first important publication was in 1799—ten years after the French Revolution had instilled in all Frenchmen an appreciation of abrupt change. Charles Lyell was the foremost 'gradualist' of the nineteenth century. Lyell was a wealthy, Oxford-educated intellectual of Georgian and Victorian England—could his scientific leanings have been influenced by the gentle, and gentlemanly, surroundings to which he was accustomed? Even today, there are some striking parallels: several of the staunchest 'punctuationists' in the United States are openly Marxist in their politics, and in the Soviet Union there is strong punctuationist support—and, of course, Marxism rests on principles of abrupt, revolutionary change which would accommodate such a view of the fossil record quite easily.

Another, perhaps clearer, example of the way in which scientific ideas are influenced by the cultural milieu is in the history of technology. There has been an almost one-to-one correlation between the growth of sophistication in machines and the complexity of the models scientists use to understand the world. Galileo's conception of the solar system bears a strong resemblance to the workings of a sixteenth-century clock. The development of computers in this century has been paralleled by the use of Information Theory and Systems Analysis in understanding quite unrelated areas—from immunology to neuroanatomy. There is a direct relation between Malthus's theory of economics (*circa* 1800) and Darwin's own interpretation of natural selection and the 'economy' of nature (in fact Darwin openly credited Malthus for his inspiration).

Of course the fact that scientific advances can be influenced, or even determined, by cultural, political, or philosophical conditions does not mean that these advances are bound to be wrong; we don't think Galileo was wrong about the solar system just because he may have got inspiration from a clock. What this does imply is that we should not jump to premature conclusions about nature; when there are differences of opinion we should look closely at the facts and be aware that interpretation may be influenced almost unconsciously by other factors. A fresh perspective may be just around the corner!

The loss of confidence in neo-Darwinism arises, therefore, from two separate sources. On the one hand a growing number of biologists are rethinking and modifying the existing theory; on the other hand this identity crisis is only one aspect of a much larger phenomenon—an awareness among 'new' scientists that science is fallible after all, that it may not have all the answers.

Where does this leave Darwin and neo-Darwinism? Can the existing theory be modified to accommodate the new results, the new attitudes? Is the current fashion for anti-reductionism, and even anti-science, just that—a *fashion* which will pass? Or is neo-Darwinism about to be replaced by a new, broader theory of evolution?

Chapter 11

Darwin in descent?

———————————— ✲ ————————————

> Darwinism, then, as the natural selection of the fit, the final
> arbiter in descent control, stands unscathed, clear and high
> above the obscuring cloud of battle. At least, so it seems
> to me. But Darwinism, as the all-sufficient or even most
> important causo-mechanical factor in species-forming and
> hence as the sufficient explanation of descent, is discredited
> and cast down. . . . But Darwin himself claimed no
> *Allmacht* for selection. Darwin may well cry to be saved from
> his friends!
>
> *Vernon Kellogg, 1907*

It is somehow apt that the conclusion which I think should be
reached about neo-Darwinism today is very similar to a
conclusion which the American zoologist Vernon Kellogg
reached about Darwinism in 1907—seventy-five years ago.
Apt because the roots of all the present doubts can clearly be
traced to Darwin himself and frequently even earlier; perhaps
we forget too easily that truly original thoughts are few and
far between. Although Kellogg (writing *Darwinism Today*)
lacked the knowledge which recent researchers have
revealed, and despite the fact that he reached his conclusions
for slightly different reasons, I feel that he identified some of
the weaknesses in Darwinism which are at the heart of the
present debate.

Ironically, Darwin himself may be the reason that
Darwinism survives. It *is* his friends, the Darwinists and
neo-Darwinists, who sometimes do him the greatest
disservice. Unlike so many of his disciples who, in their zeal,
have overstated and clung to dogma, Darwin was
undogmatic and pluralistic in his approach. He openly

admitted the possibility of Lamarckism, or of variable rates of evolution, and he even questioned the omnipotence of selection itself in shaping change. Compare Julian Huxley's over-confidence in the last chapter with this comment from the introduction to the first edition of *The Origin of Species:*

> I am convinced that natural selection has been the main but not the exclusive means of modification.
>
> *Darwin, 1859*

Although Darwin was convinced by natural selection his books are littered with such comments—admissions of ignorance and readiness to see new perspectives. The trouble is that Darwin's hypothesis became a virtual religion in the hands of his disciples; the openness and flexibility which characterized Darwin have been lost in many of his followers.

Present-day neo-Darwinism is flexible also—it is certainly more flexible than the modern synthesis days of the 1940s and 1950s. It does not deny neutral genes, or variable rates of evolution, or even abrupt speciation by chromosome changes. It recognizes the complex reality. As long as it realizes its limitations, as long as it does not try to explain *everything* (thereby actually explaining nothing), it will remain powerful. One thing is certain: there is at present no coherent alternative to neo-Darwinism. Particular joints in the existing structure may be straining and creaking under the load of recent ideas, but at least the structure still stands. That is something no rival theory can claim.

But the naïve omniscience must go. Neo-Darwinism is an incredibly ambitious attempt to explain nature and in many respects it is simply not up to the task. As we have seen there are problems, contradictions, and new discoveries which do not sit easily in the present framework; certainly the mechanistic and gradualistic model that reigned supreme thirty years ago is no longer sufficient.

Evolution can be observed and measured at three fairly distinct levels: subspecific, specific, and superspecific. The subspecific level concerns populations of creatures and attempts to understand selection acting on variation to produce *adaptations* to the environment. The specific level deals with the events of *speciation*, the mechanics of the origin of species. The superspecific level—the *macroevolution* level—deals with the large-scale patterns of appearance and extinction, and of species-interaction, which are accessible through ecology and palaeontology. To a neo-Darwinist these distinctions are arbitrary and unnecessary because the single unifying principle of natural selection should bind the levels into one whole phenomenon explicable at all levels using the same terms and principles. Naturally it would be a great advance if this unification was justified—but is it?

I think the neo-Darwinists have been hypnotized by the elegance of their theory, and by the promise of unity, prematurely. Can our understanding of adaptation *explain* speciation? Not yet. Does natural selection *predict* the patterns of the fossil record? No. Let us look more closely at the three levels.

First, at the subspecific level, there is strong evidence for the power of selection. Our best explanation for adaptation is natural selection. Yet even at this level there are complications. Is 'neutralism' common? Is there *any* Lamarckian inheritance? What role does development play in aiding adaptation? At this level neo-Darwinism stands as the 'best bet' theory to explain observations, with the proviso that there are still some embarrassing gaps in the story.

Second, at the specific level, natural selection looks rather weak. If adaptation *necessarily* led to speciation then natural selection could safely be called the cause of the origin of species, but it does not. Many of the events which seem to be associated with speciation—geographic isolation, chromosome duplications and rearrangements, repetitive DNA sequences, even neoteny—have little to do with natural selection. At this level natural selection is compatible with observation but is in no sense a sufficient explanation of speciation.

Third, at the superspecific level, natural selection seems further weakened. Although it is possible to reconcile neo-Darwinism with either gradualism or punctuationism in the fossil record, the theory is incapable of predicting *which* of these large-scale patterns will be found and in that sense it is somehow irrelevant to the superspecific observations. The palaeontologists' new *cri de coeur*—that macroevolution be uncoupled from microevolution—seems reasonable.

This is not to say that the neo-Darwinian synthesis is wrong; just that clinging to neo-Darwinism alone may actually impede the progress of biology, and our understanding of evolution, by the pretension that we can explain more than we actually can. After all, what explorer heads into terrain for which there is already rumoured to be a map? How can biologists ask fresh questions about evolution if the neo-Darwinists keep pretending they have all the answers? Very few of the new experiments discussed in this book cannot be reconciled with the existing theory—it is possible to modify and expand neo-Darwinism into all sorts of shapes. But the theory is insufficient to explain and predict these new observations, and it must therefore be 'reduced to size' accordingly.

I think neo-Darwinism will survive as the best existing theory of adaptation, but that its importance as a theory of speciation—an explanation for the origin of species—and in understanding the large-scale events of evolution will be diminished. In some fields the idea of natural selection may turn out to be irrelevant or unilluminating. Even in those areas where it remains the best explanation—in particular population genetics—there will almost certainly be shifts in emphasis due to the present attacks:

1. The neo-Darwinists should look again at the possibilities of rapid, abrupt morphological change. Whether by switch genes, or by alterations in developmental timing, or even by sudden genetic revolutions, there are some interesting possible mechanisms for achieving significant bodily changes; these are well worth investigation. The Darwinists have emphasized gradualism for too long.

2. What does 'random' really mean? One of the mainstays of neo-Darwinism is the notion of 'random variants', mutations, which selection may then act upon. But is the origin of variation a truly chance phenomenon? How can the obvious co-ordination of an adaptive response arise from unconnected chance events? For too long the

word 'random' seems to have really meant 'poorly understood'; this part of the synthesis needs clarifying.

3. Neo-Darwinism must acknowledge that some crucial pieces in the jigsaw puzzle are still missing. The pathway of development from genes to whole creatures still remains a mystery, and we cannot assume that when this is fully understood it will fall neatly into place beside other aspects of the theory; the chances are that a knowledge of development will fundamentally alter our understanding of adaptation.

4. How objective a science is neo-Darwinism? History can furnish some dramatic examples of culture, politics, or philosophy influencing science; Darwinism itself has some striking parallels in the history of politics and economics. Once again this does not necessarily mean that the ideas prompted by external events are mistaken, but it does imply that pure research is rarely pure. Are there alternative theories which could explain the observations just as well?

5. Finally, neo-Darwinism should make room for a less reductionist, less atomistic approach to nature. Everywhere we look nature is manifested as integrated 'wholeness', and co-ordination; yet the scientific method is by definition analytic and piecemeal. In some cases this has succeeded admirably, but in others it has not. Evolution spans so many levels in the hierarchy of nature (molecules to organs, individuals to mass extinctions) that the neo-Darwinists must realize the inherent danger of applying the same rules at all levels. A phenomenon which may appear random at one level (the toss of a coin, for example) is actually causal and non-random at a different level (if we could measure all the minute forces acting on the coin we could predict its fall).

This is not a plea for mysticism or a tirade against science. Science is the single most reliable tool at our disposal for reaching an understanding of nature. But if it becomes a religion, if it becomes the only pair of glasses through which we view the world, we are in danger of not seeing the wood for the trees. So the reductionism or the atomism of the neo-

Darwin in descent?

Darwinists has in some cases obscured the reality; the questions we have asked of nature have been those for which we could envisage an answer. There is certainly more to reality than that.

Evolutionary theory is in a state of flux. By the time the research of the past few years has been assimilated we may well see a major shift in our understanding. That shift will, I think, reduce the importance of natural selection and hence neo-Darwinism. It is not that the theory will be found to be inherently faulty—it will become only one aspect of a much larger and more general theory of evolution.

References

❀

BATESON, G. 1963. The rate of somatic change in evolution. *Evolution 17*, 520-39.

CHARLESWORTH, B. *et al.* 1982. In defence of neo-Darwinism. In press.

DARWIN, CHARLES 1859. *The Origin of Species.* John Murray, London.

DARWIN, CHARLES 1872. *The Expression of the Emotions in Man and Animals.* John Murray, London.

DARWIN, ERASMUS 1794. *Zoonomia.* P. Byrne, Dublin.

DAWKINS, R. 1976. *The Selfish Gene.* Oxford University Press, Oxford.

DE VRIES, H. 1906. *Species and Varieties: their origin by mutation etc.* Chicago.

DOBZHANSKY, Th. 1970. *Genetics of the Evolutionary Process.* Columbia University Press, New York.

DOVER, G. *et al.* 1980. Springcleaning ribosomal DNA . . . *Nature 290,* 731-2.

FOREY, P. 1981. *Introduction to Cladistics.* In press.

GOLDSCHMIDT, R. 1940. *The Material Basis of Evolution.* Yale University Press, New Haven, Conn.

GOODENOUGH, U. & LEVINE, R. P. 1975. *Genetics.* Holt, Rinehart & Winston, London.

GOODWIN, B. C. 1978. Pattern formation and its regeneration in the protozoa. *Soc. Gen. Microbiol. 30,* 377-404.

GOULD, S. J. 1978. Return of the hopeful monster. In *Natural History* (later in *The Panda's Thumb*, W. W. Norton, 1981).

GOULD, S. J. & LEWONTIN, R. C. 1979. The spandrels of San Marco and the Panglossian paradigm: a critique of the adaptationist program. *Proc. Roy. Soc. Lond., series B 205,* 581-98.

GOULD, S. J. 1980. Quoted in 'Evolutionary theory under fire'. *Science 210,* 883-7.

References

GOULD, S. J. 1980. Is a new and general theory of evolution emerging? *Palaeobiology 6(1)*, 119-130.

GOULD, S. J. 1981. In *Evolution and Development*. (Bonner, J. T., ed.) (Dahlem.) Springer-Verlag, Berlin.

HAECKEL, E. 1905. *The Evolution of Man*. (2 Vols.) (McCabe, J., tr.) From fifth edition of *Anthropogenie*. Watts & Co., London.

HALLAM, A. (ed.) 1977. *Patterns of Evolution*, Elsevier, Oxford.

HALLAM, A. 1981. Letter in *London Review of Books*, 18 June 1981, p. 10.

HALSTEAD, B. 1980. Letter in *Nature 288*, 208.

HANSON, N. 1958. *Patterns of Discovery*. Cambridge University Press, Cambridge.

HUXLEY, J. 1942. *Evolution. The Modern Synthesis*. Allen & Unwin, London.

HUXLEY, J. 1953. *Evolution in Action*. Chatto & Windus, London.

JEFFREYS, A. 1981. Evolution of globin gene clusters. Paper in Genome Evolution Conference, Cambridge.

KELLOGG, V. 1907. *Darwinism Today*. Bell & Sons, London.

KIMURA, M. 1977. The neutral theory of evolution. *Scientific American*, March.

LAMARCK, J. B. de 1809. *Philosophie Zoologique*. (2 Vols.) Paris.

LEAKEY, R. 1981. *The Making of Mankind*. BBC Television.

LEWONTIN, R. C. 1974. *The Genetic Basis of Evolutionary Change*. Columbia University Press, New York.

LEWONTIN, R. C. 1980. Quoted by Hallam, A., in *London Review of Books*, 16 July 1981, p. 4.

LINNAEUS, C. 1735. *Systema Naturae*.

LYELL, C. 1830-3. *Principles of Geology*. (3 Vols.) John Murray, London.

MADDOX, J. 1981. In *Nature 289*, 735.

MATHEW, P. 1831. *On Naval Timber and Arboriculture*. London.

MAYNARD SMITH, J. 1966. *The Theory of Evolution*. (Second edition.) Penguin Books, London.

MAYNARD SMITH, J. 1980. Macroevolution. *Nature 289*, 13-14.

MAYNARD SMITH, J. 1981. In *London Review of Books*, 18 June 1981, p. 11.

MAYR, E. 1963. *Animal Species and Evolution*. Belknap Press, Harvard, Mass.

McDOUGALL, W. 1927. An experiment for testing the hypothesis of Lamarck. *Brit. J. Psych. 17*, 267-304.

MORGAN, T. H. 1915. *A Critique of the Theory of Evolution*. Princetown University Press, New Jersey.

References

MORRIS, H. 1978. *The Twilight of Evolution*. Baker Book House, Grand Rapids, Michigan.

OLDROYD, D. R. 1980. *Darwinian Impacts*. Open University Press, Milton Keynes.

OSTER, G. 1980. The mechanical basis of morphogenesis. *Dev. Biol. 85*, 1-17.

PATTERSON, C. 1980. Cladistics. *Biologist 27*, 234-40.

PATTERSON, C. 1981. In 'Are the reports of Darwin's death exaggerated?'. BBC Radio 4, October.

PLATNICK, N. 1980. Philosophy and the transformation of cladistics. *Systematic Zoology 28*, 537-46.

POPPER, K. 1959. *The Logic of Scientific Discovery*. Hutchinson, London.

POPPER, K. 1974. *Unending Quest*, Fontana, London.

ROMANES, G. J. 1897. *The Life and Letters of G. J. Romanes*. (Romanes, E., ed.) Longman & Green, London.

SCHOPF, T. 1977. In *Patterns of Evolution*. (Hallam, A., ed.) Elsevier, Oxford.

SEEBOHM, H. 1888. *Physiological Selection*.

SHELDRAKE, R. 1981. *A New Science of Life*. Blond & Briggs, London.

STEBBINS, G. L. & AYALA, F. J. 1981. Is a new evolutionary synthesis necessary? *Science 213*, 967.

STEELE, E. J. 1979. *Somatic Selection and Adaptive Evolution*. Williams & Wallace, Toronto.

STEELE, E. J. & GORCZYNSKI, R. 1980. *Proc. Nat. Acad. Sci. USA 77*, 2871.

STENT, G. 1981. In *Evolution and Development*. (Bonner, J. T., ed.) Springer-Verlag, Berlin.

TEMIN, H. 1971. The protovirus hypothesis... *J. National Cancer Inst. 46*.

THOMPSON, D'ARCY W. 1942. *On Growth and Form*. Cambridge University Press, Cambridge.

WADDINGTON, C. H. 1957. *The Strategy of the Genes*. Allen & Unwin, London.

WHITE, M. 1978. *Modes of Speciation*. Freeman, Reading.

WOLPERT, L. 1978. Pattern formation in biological development. *Scientific American*, October.

ZUCKERKANDL, E. 1978. Programs of gene action and progressive evolution. In *Molecular Anthropolgy*. Plenum Press, New York.

Illustration sources

Figures 1, 4 and 5, from *Origin of Species*, The British Museum (Natural History); figure 2, from *Scientific American*, November 1979; figure 7, from S. J. Gould, *Ontogeny and Phylogeny*, Harvard University Press; figure 10, from Francis Hitching, *The Neck of the Giraffe, or Where Darwin Went Wrong*, Pan Books; figure 11, from *The British Journal of Psychiatry*; figure 12, from A. S. Romer and T. S. Parsons, *The Vertebrate Body* (fifth edition). Copyright 1977 by W. B. Saunders Company. Copyright 1970, 1962, 1955, and 1949 by W. B. Saunders Company. Reprinted by permission of Holt, Rinehart and Winston, CBS College Publishing. Figure 13, from *Scientific American*, October 1978; figure 14, from J. Needham, *Biochemistry and Morphogenesis*, Cambridge University Press; figures 15 and 16, from C. H. Waddington, *The Strategy of the Genes*, George Allen & Unwin; figure 17, from N. R. Hanson, *Patterns of Discovery*, Cambridge University Press; figure 18, from E. Haeckel, *The Evolution of Man*, Watts & Co.; figures 20 and 21, from D'Arcy W. Thompson, *On Growth and Form*, Cambridge University Press. Figures 1, 3, 6, 7, 18 and 19 were drawn by Joan Sellwood.

Index

Index

172

Index

173

Index